ART

—OF THE—

WINE LABEL

ROBERT JOSEPH

ART
— OF THE —
WINE
LABEL

ROBERT JOSEPH

WINDWARD

A QUARTO BOOK

Windward
an imprint owned by W H Smith and Son Limited
Registered no 237811 England
Trading as W H Smith Distributors
St John's House, East Street, Leicester, LE1 6NE

ISBN 0 71120 48 29

This book was designed and produced by
Quarto Publishing plc
The Old Brewery, 6 Blundell Street
London N7 9BH

Senior Editor: Polly Powell
Editor: Henrietta Wilkinson

Designers: Bob Cocker, Hazel Edington, Ursula Dawson
Photographer: John Heseltine

Art Director: Moira Clinch
Editorial Director: Carolyn King

Special thanks to Joanna Bradshaw, Jacky Morley and
Laura Beck

Typeset by QV Typesetting Ltd
Manufactured in Hong Kong by Regent Publishing
Services Ltd
Printed by Leefung-Asco Printers Ltd, Hong Kong

Quarto Publishing would like to thank Robert Opie of the
Museum of Advertising and Packaging in Gloucester and
Gilles Larrue of the Association Nationale d'Oenographilie for
allowing labels from their collections to be included
in this book.

CONTENTS

FOREWORD

I HAVE been fascinated by paper wine labels since long before I was ever allowed to develop a taste for the contents of the bottles they adorned. Why, I used to wonder, were some so different from others? How did people know that Château This was from one place whereas Château That was from somewhere completely different? Did all this gold on the label really indicate a classier wine? And what did all those words mean? Over the years, this fascination has grown as I have discovered new wines and new labels from a wide range of countries.

To a wine writer or a wine lover, the most important factor of any wine has to be the flavour. The label is just the frame around the painting; without it, the wine would taste just as good — or bad. I have come across glorious wines which are less attractively labelled than some furniture polish. But I have also had the misfortune to taste absolute dross dressed up to look like royalty. Occasionally, there have been bottles which have left me

wishing that the label designer had been responsible for producing the wine; he — or she — so evidently has better taste than
the winemaker.

I have enormously enjoyed writing this book. I hope that the
labels which appear on these pages give you as much pleasure
as they have given me.

I want to thank, for their help, encouragement and, in
several cases, valuable assistance in obtaining hard-to-find
labels, Maureen Ashley MW, Richard Hobson MW, David Gleave
MW, Jacquie Kay, Cindy Brunck, Marilyn Draper, Fiona Wild and
Charles Metcalfe.

My particular thanks must go to Claude Clevenot, Tim
Stanley-Clarke, Christian Bizot of Bollinger, Joanna Simon of
WINE Magazine, Margaret Rand of *Wine and Spirit* and Avril
Stubbs of Ostlers. The contribution of Juliette Avis was crucial
and Christina Ker Gibson was as forbearing as ever.

HISTORY
OF THE
LABEL

WINE labels are rather like passports, descriptive documents without which it is difficult to travel very far; and, like passports, wine labels are a comparatively recent invention. Until 200 or so years ago, men either crossed frontiers as part of an army, or rarely crossed them at all; those who had the means and freedom to do so rarely needed officially endorsed identity documents. Much the same could be said of wine; it was either transported in barrels, or it remained in the region in which it was produced. From the barrel it would be served in jugs of one kind or another, so what need was there for a bottle-label?

Curiously, however, a form of wine labelling was in use thousands of years ago, providing we are prepared to treat the word "label" reasonably loosely. The very oldest "label" anyone has been able to authenticate is a 6,000 year-old Babylonian cylindrical seal which was used to mark amphorae. Appropriately enough, and not unlike some wine advertisements today, it depicted a group of jolly looking people all becoming jollier with the help of a flask or two of fermented grape juice.

Other cylinders and tablets of the same period prove how much the Egyptians understood about both wine and beer making, and show the way in which amphorae were marked. Sadly, though, none of the amphorae themselves have survived, and it is to the Romans and Greeks that we have to look for the first confirmation that the identity of a wine was as important as its flavour. The Romans imprinted their amphorae with the name of the wine and of the consul under whose rule it was made and, if one is to believe Pliny the Younger, some of them at least took care to sort one *cuvée* from another:

"I...supped lately with a person who...had apportioned in small flagons three different sorts of wine...One was for himself and me; the next for his friends of a lower order..; and the third for

his own freed-men and mine."

According to Bob Woodward and Carl Bernstein in their book *All the President's Men*, Richard Nixon behaved very similarly 2,000 years later, serving visiting congressmen "a rather good, six-dollar wine" while he enjoyed "his favourite, a 1966 Château Margaux which sold for about $30 a bottle". Needless to say, none of the guests ever saw the label of the Margaux, since the President took care to have it wrapped in a towel.

Nixon's behaviour — some would call it mean, others sensible — would have made sense to a great many wine drinkers through the ages, but up until this century, there would have been no need for a towel. Wine, or at any rate good wine, rarely came to the dining table in a bottle; a jug of — usually red — wine would be drawn off from a barrel and poured directly into guests' glasses. Sometimes it would be nectar, sometimes it would be vinegar; either way, its name would not be an issue.

An early example of a glass "label" on a bottle. Unlike a silver decanter label, this shows the ownership of the bottle and its contents. In this respect, it is very similar to a Roman amphora.

Although the barrels had identifying marks of one kind or another, these too were treated casually. The name of a wine often owed more to the place where it was bought than to where its vines were grown. The "great black wine" of Cahors, for example, was shipped from Bordeaux, and so it was known as Bordeaux even though the two wines have little in common, as anyone who has tasted Cahors will know. In Burgundy, Pommard was the site of a regular market where the wines of the neighbouring village of Volnay were sold, and by which name they were known. It was a rare 17th-century wine drinker who would look quizzically at his flagon and say, "forsooth, this is no Pommard that I see before me, but a Volnay!"

WINE JUGS

In the Middle Ages, particularly in Europe, most wine was served in earthenware jugs which came in two forms: tall and saggily egg-shaped, perhaps as an echo of the leather wine bottle of the time, and wider and squatter, decorated with lattice-work patterns. Between the 13th and 16th centuries the production of these jugs improved with better quality glazes, although they still did not bear the name of the wine they contained. But this anonymity is not particularly surprising. The name of the wine would have been of as little interest to the drinkers as that of the ale being swigged at the same tables. And besides, jugs were refilled from the barrel at such a rate that there could have been little guarantee that the wine on Monday came from the same source as that on Friday. In their way, these jugs were predecessors of the more modern decanters rather than of wine bottles as we know them today.

As decorative styles became still more elaborate, under the influence of Turkish pottery, Chinese porcelain and Venetian glass, lettering became at once more and less possible. Had anyone wanted to mark the name of a wine onto a jug, they might have done so, but the ornate decoration left them too little space.

During the late 15th and 16th centuries, however, the Italians developed the art of tin-enamelling pottery and of producing brightly coloured lettering and designs. This expertise migrated northwards to Antwerp and Delft, where painted wine jugs soon became art forms in themselves.

The "Lambeth jugs" produced in England between 1639-1672 reveal a taste for four styles of wine: Claret, Whit (white wine), Rhenish and, most popular of all, Sack. They also prove an appreciation of the importance of vintages, as is shown by the "1641 Rhenish" jug on show at the British Museum in London.

At one time, it was thought that these jugs were the precursors of the modern bottle, and that they were used to store wine in the 17th-century cellar. But as N.M. Penzer explains in his *Book of the Wine Label*, this theory does not really make sense; the jugs were both too expensively produced and too small for

As well as a bottle and a decanter, this photograph shows a 17th-century
Sack jug, typical of ones used widely in Britain at that time.

A selection of silver champagne labels, complete with numerous misspellings.

such a use. In his opinion, they were a further step towards the decanter — *"vessels used in well-to-do private households for the tabling of their wines"*. And it was a short step from the printing of wine names on jugs to the invention of the silver and the enamel wine label.

SILVER AND ENAMEL LABELS

Dating from the 18th and 19th centuries, these labels were essentially an English device, allowing a gentleman to present his guests with two or more decanters of wine, each bearing a kind of luxurious identity tag. The accuracy of these silver labels, however, often left much to be desired. As Penzer says, mistakes occurred either

"in the country of origin due to wrongly transcribing the name which has only been heard and not seen written... [or to the fact that] *the customer...may have given the order* [for engraving] *from abroad during his travels, and one can well imagine curious and unknown words and a thick quill pen being responsible for many mistakes"*.

Considerable, although misplaced, effort must have gone into engraving *Popt* (presumably for a Port), *Champagn* and *Champaigne*, not to mention *Clarrette, Clarrett* and *Clart*. Some spellings are so bizarre that one can only guess at their meaning: *Voluaij* was probably Volnay, but what on earth was, or were, *Bottoms?* They may well have been the lees from the bottom of wine casks, though who would want a decanter label for such undrinkable stuff is anyone's guess.

PAPER LABELS

The first apparent evidence of a paper label is to be found on an old bottle in the Pfalz-Museum in Speyer, W. Germany. The handwritten words on faded paper read "Steinwin, 1631er", but the effect, and authenticity, are somewhat spoiled by the attractive crown on the top of the label which is lithographically printed. Lithography was not invented until 1798...

Moët & Chandon are proud to show off bottles labelled "Mousseux Claude Moët", 1741 and 1745. The bottles are

unquestionably 200 years old but, as Belgian author Georges Renoy points out in his book *Les Etiquettes du Vin*, the handwriting style and the crossed sevens of the handwritten labels seem more typical of the 19th than of the 18th century.

For the first certain indication of the existence of handwritten labels, one has to turn to the helpfully precise illustrations of William Hogarth. In his *An Election Entertainment (Number 1)* which dates from 1755, three bottles appear to bear parchment labels with the handwritten words Gin, Burgundy and Champagne. Even so, it is fair to assume that such labelling was rare, and although various other kinds of labels have been found from this period, no wine labels have survived.

Bordeaux labels from the late 19th century, indicating the wine's style but neither château name nor vintage. German labels of a similar age, also making no mention of the producer's name.

The oldest labels to be seen are those in the *Musée du Vin* at Beaune from 1798, two bottles labelled 1800 at Pauillac (the labels are printed, but the vintage is handwritten) and a pretty, floral, orange and blue Liebfraumilch (or rather *Liebfrauen-milch*) label of the same year. With the latter, the wine producer, one Theodor Brass, had evidently economised by having the "18" printed, leaving a space for the two zeros to be added in by hand. This German label may have been one of the first to be produced on the new lithographic printing presses invented by Alois Senefelder two years earlier, and installed in a nearby printing works for Johann Anton Andre. Other German labels of this era still exist, many differing from those of Theodor Brass by not including the name of the producer. Presumably, as still happens today, various producers of Niersteiner would use the same labels.

By 1830 the production of labels for German wine had stepped up enormously, and there were already opportunities for artists to create individual styles. In the mid 1800s, Champagne, a French region whose wines were beginning to enjoy widespread popularity, also started to produce a variety of dazzlingly luxurious labels. Gold, silver, bronze, rich blues and russets all helped to affirm the status of the sparkling wine, and particularly of houses such as Bollinger, Lanson and Mumm.

In a sense, these champagne labels defined the role of the wine label from the mid 19th to the mid 20th centuries. There

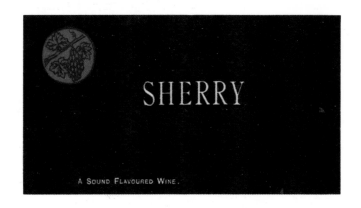

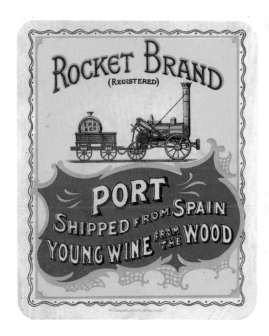

ABOVE: *Examples of sherry and port labels used to describe wines which bore no resemblance to the real thing. Note that the Rocket brand of port comes from Spain rather than Portugal.* OPPOSITE: *Three labels which are illegal under EEC law. The Australian "claret" is made from the same grape varieties as the wines of the Rhône whereas the Portuguese "St. Julian" alludes to the Bordeaux commune of St. Julien. There is no such wine as Chaban* premier cru *— this bottle dates from the days of "declassified" Burgundy; it might contain Chablis* premier cru.

was no point in producing ornate labels for wines whose bottles would never be seen, but a memorable label could make all the difference to those wines which were not only opened "at table", but which also benefitted from advertising.

Several champagne houses have recently revived the label styles of a century ago, but contemporary standards of crafts-manship are rarely as fine as they were then. The nearest equiv-alent today would be the production of a limited-edition print.

BOTTLED WINE

The next step in the evolution of the wine label came with the increase in the sale of bottled wine. Champagne, by definition, has always had to be poured straight from the bottle, but the move towards château bottling in Bordeaux created a need for the same kind of individual labels as those being used in Reims and Epernay. The Industrial Revolution led to the birth of a new wine drinking class who ordered wines from the lists offered in the increasingly successful restaurants of the late 19th and early 20th centuries.

These early labels were not bound by restrictions or oblig-ations; they could include or exclude as much information as they pleased. The first laws covering wine labels date from the

ABOVE: The vibrant colours of the de Renaudin Bollinger label would be difficult to recapture today, but Bollinger's own embossed 1981 Vieilles Vignes Françaises is very much in the style of a century ago. OPPOSITE: Note the mention of the now defunct Deuxième Zone on the Chaurey Fils, and of the village of Sillery on the Moët & Chandon bottle.

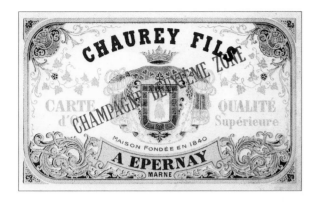

introduction of legally designated wine regions in various countries during the first half of this century. With them came the requirement to include particular pieces of information, and to respect certain specified criteria. In France, for example, there is even a ruling which covers the weight of paper on which the labels are printed. In Italy, these newer pieces of labelling legislation are often ignored by winemakers and designers who see no reason for being restricted in their wine labelling.

LABEL CRIME

Thanks to the plethora of laws which exist in every winemaking nation nowadays, any contemporary wine label *should* give a pretty clear idea of both the provenance of the wine and, ideally, its quality. This was not the case in the past.

Just over 60 years ago, the forthright wine writer, Morton Shand, declared:

"Though by the law of France, no wine may bear the name of Bordeaux which was not made from grapes grown in the département *of the Gironde, it must not be forgotten that the town of Cette* [now known as Sète] *— to choose the most glaring instance — is a very Sodom and Gomorrah of vinous iniquity, where by judicious blending with hot and inferior wines from Algeria and the Midi or Benicarlo from Spain, together with a little "scientific" aftercare, any and every variety of wine, from British* [by which is meant the national palate in] *Beaune to French Port, can be readily 'produced'* [that is, manufactured]. *In 1897,*

between 500 and 600,000 hectolitres [60-80 *million* bottles] *of liquids falsely described as foreign wines* [such as Port, Sherry, Malaga, Madeira, Cyprus, Samos and Marsala] *were despatched from Cette. It used to be said that you could order 50 hogsheads apiece of Port, Sherry and Bordeaux at 9 a.m. and take delivery of the finished mixture at 4 p.m. the same day".*

The practices Morton Shand described in 1926 were by no means new. In 1837, Stendahl, author of *Le Rouge et Le Noir,* wrote of:

"A lodge or manufactory of wines. With wine, sugar, iron-filings, and certain floral essences they make here the wines of all

countries"— nor, sadly, was it wholly eradicated with the introduction of *Appellation Contrôlée* in 1936.

To begin with, *Appellation Contrôlée* only applied to wines sold within the EEC. At the end of the 1960s, the London *Sunday Times* revealed just how little of the wine sold in Britain as Beaujolais had in fact come from that region. Even when Britain joined the EEC in the early 1970s, and subjected its wine trade to the strict laws which were in force in France, there was no absolute guarantee that a wine label told the truth.

In 1972, the wine world erupted with the news that the previously highly respected Bordeaux firm of Cruse was charged

While many Bordeaux châteaux have maintained the same labels since they began bottling early this century, Léoville Barton's designs have altered radically. The label on the left is from the 1937 vintage, but it was still being used in the 1950s. The 1985 label is the first to use a recently commissioned print of the château.

with using wine from the Midi in the production of huge quantities of "Bordeaux type", "Côtes-du-Rhône type" and "Burgundy type" wine, sold with *Appellation Contrôlée* labels as if they were the real thing. At the time, a rash of "after the Bordeaux trial" wine jokes emerged, one of which referred to Japanese wine labelled "Beware of French imitations".

In France such frauds have been mercifully rare, although early 1987 saw a Loire merchant charged with selling humble Gros Plant as Muscadet. In Austria, Germany and Italy in the mid 1980s, however, cases of wine were falsified with chemicals, with tragic consequences in some instances.

But very often, wine falsification takes place far from the vineyards. Just as Cartier has to expend great efforts on tracing the perpetrators of fake watches and jewellery, Mumm Champagne has found itself in similar pursuit of an Italian gang which was putting forged Mumm Cordon Rouge labels on cheap Italian fizz. By the same token, British wine merchants have been caught sticking new labels on old bottles on occasion, turning cheap *vin blanc* into a more valuable Bourgogne Blanc, or *vin rouge* into Claret, doubling or tripling the value of the contents in the process.

Fortunately, however, such overt frauds, like the incidence of

Beware of making assumptions - the top label is of Château Lafite, the one beneath it, of Château La Cardonne, a cheaper wine owned by the same family. The third label is of a château which is not even in Bordeaux; it has no connection with Lafite at all, and is merely borrowing the label style.

poisonously adulterated wine, are usually uncovered, thanks to the close-knit nature of the international wine trade. While it is possible to get away with this kind of fraud on a small scale, it would be very difficult to escape detection if plans became too ambitious.

LABEL DESIGN

The design of wine labels has developed into an impressive industry in recent years, despite the large number of the world's wine producers who are happy to buy traditional-style labels off-the-peg from a local printer, and to stick precisely the same label on their 1987 vintage as they did on their 1967.

The reason for this growth is easily traced. Fifty years ago, the vast majority of finer wine was either sold by the case by merchants, or poured in restaurants by wine waiters. The look of a label was important only for a few champagne houses which considered their overall image as being as important as the flavour of the wine; other winemakers were happy to rely on their own name and that of the wine to attract customers.

The explosive success of wine retailers, and wine-selling supermarkets in particular, has changed all of that. Far more people are drinking good wine than ever before, and nowadays, there are few helpful wine merchants to advise on the particular qualities and characteristics of this or that bottle. The wine has to sell itself.

Although Philippe de Rothschild's Mouton Rothschild labels had considerable influence on label design, it was arguably another wine launched in the 1930s which gave a clearer direction to the world's winemakers and merchants.

BRANDED WINES

When the German firm of H. Sichel Sohne in Mainz decided to launch a branded wine, they were straying into more or less untried territory. At the time, their Liebfraumilch Spätlese "Nun" brand took the customers of the previously highly traditionalist company by surprise; not least because when the wine was sold as "Blue Nun Label" in the 1940s the two nuns in the foreground of the label picture were both dressed in *brown*. This inconsistency was sorted out in the 1950s with a swift colour change, and more recently, the two nuns became one.

But Blue Nun has a competitor for its place as *the* long-standing wine marketing success story. If anything, Mateus Rosé deserves even greater credit because unlike the German wine, this Portuguese, medium-sweet, slightly sparkling, rosé created a new style of wine as well as a wholly new brand.

Both these wines owe their success to two factors: on the one hand, they had easy-to-read labels, requiring no effort at foreign pronunciation and regional wine knowledge; and on the other, both shared an attractively "classless" image. Until wine drinkers became more sophisticated — a recent phenomenon — ordering Blue Nun or Mateus in a shop or restaurant was a safe decision.

The unexpected success of Mateus is shown by a classic anecdote, recounted with relish by members of the Guedes family whose father created the wine. Senhor Guedes

The changing face — and colour — of Blue Nun.

approached the owner of the palace next door to the Mateus winery for permission to use a picture of his building on the label, offering either a royalty per label or a one-off payment. The aristocratic neighbour asked a few questions about the wine and learnt that it was going to be semi-sweet and would be sold in a type of bottle historically used in Franconia, in Germany (and never previously in Portugal). He then declined the royalty, reportedly shaking his head at the madness of the enterprise. The one-off payment was less than would have been paid on the royalties on the first year alone. The nobleman's only consolation has been the admission fee he has been able to charge Mateus-loving tourists who insist on visiting his home.

Another successful branded Portuguese wine is Gatão. In English, the name of this highly commercial wine means cat,

and so it is hardly surprising that on the labels of Gatão bottles sold throughout the world there is a picture of a puss-in-boots. Everywhere, that is, except for Great Britain, where the label depicts a mermaid. According to one report, "our customers don't like cats..."

The key to modern label design, however, is to capture the style and character of the wine, to provide the casual shelf-browser with an immediate impression of the flavour he or she is going to get from any one bottle. No one has achieved this more effectively than Claude Clevenot, whose Burgundian *Imprimerie du Moulin* is responsible for the floral labels which are now inseparably associated with the Beaujolais of Georges Duboeuf. When compared to the labels Duboeuf used to use — and with those which still appear on so many more traditional

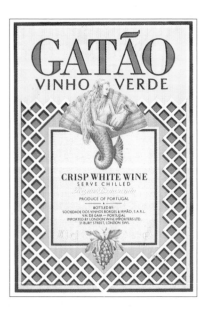

LEFT and ABOVE: In Britain, apparently, wine drinkers do not like cats; on the left, the Portuguese label used throughout the world — except in Great Britain, which gets the label on the right.
OPPOSITE: Few labels and wine names can have taken as long to devise as this one. Opus One is the co-production of Baron Philippe de Rothschild of Bordeaux and Robert Mondavi of California. The final label is a triumph of compromise.

Beaujolais wines — one can appreciate how innovative the new design has been, and how appropriate to the fresh and fruity style of the Duboeuf wines.

The Duboeuf flowers have inevitably been followed by birds, insects and landscapes for other producers from the *Imprimerie du Moulin's* team of artists. The most obvious of the Duboeuf look-alikes is to be found on the label of a big-selling wine in Australia.

BACK LABELS

If wine labels are a comparatively recent invention, "back labels" are positive newcomers. Even now, their presence is more or less restricted to winemakers in the "New World" and to a small number in Italy and Spain.

Back labels take a number of forms. At their most official, there are the maps which appear on the backs of Rioja bottles, telling you whether the wine is a *Crianza*, a *Reserva* or a *Gran Reserva*. This gives an indication of both the quality of the vintage and the number of years the wine will have spent in oak barrels. Rioja back labels are more established than those of most other countries; I have two different 1942 vintage wines, both of which have *Diploma de Garantia* back labels, explaining in Spanish that the wine they grace is genuine.

More often, however, the back labels have been written and produced by the winemaker or merchant. They can be extremely

Back labels of every kind, ranging from a straightforward Valpolicella label to a typical Californian label with plenty to say.

useful, telling you precisely where the wine comes from, how it should be served and possibly of particular characteristics to be encountered in that particular wine. Burgundies from the house of Leroy carry a label which explains that the company prefers not to filter its wine before bottling and that a fine deposit might consequently be found in the bottle. And the German wine shipper Deinhard prints a similarly helpful label on its bottles which reads:

"You will notice that there are some crystals at the bottom of this bottle. The reason for this is that certain fine wines with a high extract tend to a crystallization of tartaric acid after being bottled. It is a perfectly natural development, and in no way harms the taste of the wine".

All well and good, but what about all of those non-technical wine drinkers who are not quite certain what "high extract" and "tartaric acid" are? Those unfortunates will be even more fog-bound if they look at the back of all too many Californian wine bottles. If they do, there is a high chance that they will be told all about the "sugar at harvest" — usually referred to in *brix* — the date of the harvest, the fermentation temperature, the length of time the wine has spent in oak barrels, the forest from which the oak came (yes, I am serious) and the name of the barrel-maker.

The nonsensical aspect of this becomes clear when you realise that *brix* are not used in any of the tradititional vine-yards of Europe, so even the most highly qualified winemaker in

Bordeaux would most certainly have difficulty translating *brix* into terms he understands unless he has spent time in California. And just in case you thought that reference to a wine book might help, neither the otherwise comprehensive *Alexis Lichine Encyclopaedia of Wines and Spirits*, nor the *New York Times Book of Wine* offer any help on the subject at all. As for the harvest date, there is little use in knowing that the grapes were picked on October 5th in one vineyard without knowing the date of which others in the same region were picked.

WINE LAWS

Thankfully, legislation instigated by individual countries of Europe and, more recently, by the European Community as a whole, has begun to outlaw misleading labelling, and has created a wine world in which all labels should be blameless.

Of course, it does not always work out quite like that, as the recent scandals outlined elsewhere in this book prove. Even so, unless the wine falsifier is prepared to invent a fictitious producer, wine labels serve the essential purpose of enabling the authorities — and the very persistent individual — to trace a wine's origins.

Apart from the grower's, merchant's or cooperative's identity, the label should also reveal the contents of the bottle — which can vary from 68-75cl, though the EEC has plans to make 75cl the standard size — and the country from which it comes.

Beyond these basic pieces of information, the amount a label is legally required to carry varies enormously. A cheap *vin de table* has to declare its alcoholic strength: Château Latour does not. Also, the words are not always as unambiguous as one might hope. In France, a wine labelled "Cabernet Sauvignon" has to be made exclusively from that grape; Californian Cabernet Sauvignon, by contrast, can legally contain a generous amount of any other grape variety you — or the winemaker — may care to mention.

Some of these wrinkles may be ironed out as an ever-increasing amount of wine continues to cross international frontiers. Few winemakers like to have different labels for different countries and now that the EEC imposes a single set of rules for all of its members, labelling law is becoming more standardized. Within a very few years, for example, a bottle bought in the US and Europe will have to reveal its sulphur dioxide content.

But local and regional anomalies are bound to persist. One illogical piece of French label law, for example, undermines the Burgundian rule which permits growers and merchants to print the names of the village from which a wine comes, followed, where appropriate, by the name of the particular *Premier Cru* vineyard where its grapes were grown. Since these are well established as being among the best vineyards in the region, it is fair to assume that a Meursault "Charmes" will be better than

CALIFORNIA
CHABLIS

PAUL MASSON.
RARE PREMIUM WINES

This is a dry white wine with zest and personality. Of light straw color, it has a crisp clarity that rewards the eye as well as the palate. The fresh bouquet of this Chablis is captured by fermentation at ideally cool temperatures — saving the essence of the grape. Chill Chablis well before serving. It brings added enjoyment to light cuisine and is a delightful compliment to snacks of fruits and cheeses. ❧ Made and Bottled by Paul Masson Vineyards, Saratoga, California · Alcohol 11.5% by Volume.

A Paul Masson Chablis label. In the US, Chablis can be used to decribe most types of white wine but in France the term is restricted to wine produced in a small area.

plain Meursault. But what about Meursault "Tessons" and Meursault "Clos de la Barre"? Presumably the same applies to them, but neither name seems to feature among the list of Meursault *Premiers Crus*. That's the loophole: Burgundy growers can print the name of non-*Premier Cru* vineyards (those of no particular proven quality) on their labels in almost the same way as *Premiers Crus* as long as the print used for the non-*Premier Cru* vineyard be "less than half the height of that used for the *commune* name".

Another would-be helpful French law which forbids any producer whose address happens to be in an appellation from printing that address on the label of a *vin de table*. Thus a *négociant* whose cellars are in Beaune can put the words "Dupont, Négociant a Beaune" on the labels of any Bordeaux, Burgundy, Sancerre or whatever appellation, but only "Négociant a 2100"

on his Cuvée Rouge, in case the "Beaune" might mislead people into thinking that the cheap wine contains some Burgundy. However, there is nothing to prevent him from capitalising fully on his reputation as a Beaune merchant. The House of Patriarche gains enormous publicity for its purchases at the annual Hospices de Beaune charity auction — which can do no harm when it comes to selling its "Pere Patriarche" (not a drop of which has to come from Burgundy) on supermarket shelves.

The more internationally one looks, the greater the anomalies. In Europe, champagne is wine made by the *Méthode Champenoise* in the region from which it takes its name; in Australia, it can also be made by the cheaper, alternative "transfer method", and it can be produced literally anywhere; and in the US, if you want to label a bottle of lemonade "champagne", there is very little to stop you.

HOW TO
READ THE
LABEL

France has the best system of wine laws and consequently of wine labelling in the world. While there are inevitable anomalies — wines which either transcend their "class", or fail to live up to their appellation — almost every French wine should provide a reasonably clear idea of its quality and style via its label.

As a general rule, the French legal and labelling system is based on a hierarchical pyramid. At the summit there are the _grands crus_, further divided in the Médoc into first, second, third, fourth and fifth growths, or _crus_. Beneath these, or instead of them, some regions have _premiers crus_, which should be marginally better than _commune_ wines, from specifically named villages. Further down the pyramid come the regional designations, ranging from the fairly precise Beaujolais villages to the enormous Bordeaux area. In every case, while the type of grapes used and the winemaking styles will have been dictated by law, the essential quality of the wine comes from the particular character (climate or soil, for example) of specific vineyards and regions.

Alsace: principally white wine region

AOC (Appellation d'Origine Contrôlée): quality control designation for the best wines, guaranteeing provenance and grape variety

Blanc de Blancs: white wine made from white grapes — usually sparkling

Bordeaux: red and white wine region

Bourgogne: red and white wine region

Brut: dry

Brut zéro/sauvage/intégral: bone dry — used to describe champagne

Cabernet Sauvignon: red grape variety — used particularly for Bordeaux

Cave: cellar

Cave coopérative: cooperative

Cépage: grape variety

Chai: cellar — usually Bordeaux

Chardonnay: white grape variety — Burgundy, champagne

Château: any wine estate with a building

Claret: red Bordeaux

CM (Coopérative-manipulant): code on champagne label for wine made by a cooperative

Côte/Coteaux: hillside

Crémant: in champagne, less fizzy than usual wine; otherwise AOC sparkling wine made by _méthode champenoise_

Cru bourgeois: Bordeaux just beneath the _cru classé_ level

Cru classé: Bordeaux classified historically as of a certain quality, eg first, second, third growth

Cuve close: sparkling wine made by the tank method

Cuvée: selected vat

Domaine: any wine estate

Doux: sweet

Edelzwicker: Alsace blended wine

Extra dry: champagne — less dry than *sec*!

Gewürztraminer: Alsace grape

Grand cru: the best or one of the best vineyards in a particular *commune*

Vin gris/Gris de gris: pale rosé

MA (Marque Auxiliaire): champagne labelled under a secondary brand

Marque déposée: trademark

Méthode champenoise: soon-to-be-outlawed description of wine made by the champagne method

Millésime: vintage

Mise en bouteille: bottled

Moelleux: sweet

Négociant (négociant-éléveur): merchant

NM (négociant-manipulant): champagne made by a large *négociant* — ie all famous champagne

Nouveau: wine sold within months of the harvest — eg Beaujolais

Perle: slightly sparkling

Pétillant: slightly sparkling

Pinot Noir: red grape, principally in Burgundy

Premier cru: a better vineyard

Primeur: see *nouveau*

RD (récemment dégorge): champagne left on its yeast for longer than usual

RM (récoltant-manipulant): champagne made by an individual grower

Sec: dry but less dry than brut in champagne

Sélection: by itself, meaningless, but as...

Sélection de grains nobles: late harvest (Alsace), an indication of sweet quality

Supérieur: an AOC with 1% more alcohol

Sur lie: bottled on its yeast — usually Muscadet

Sylvaner: Alsace grapes

Syrah: Rhône red grapes

Tokay: Alsace name for Pinot Gris grapes

Vendange tardive: late harvest (Alsace)

Villages: AOC for best part of the appellation — eg Beaujolais Villages

Vin de pays: country wine

Vin de table: basic wine

VDQS (vin délimité de qualité supérieur): quality level between *vin de pays* and *Appellation Contrôlée*

Vin doux naturel: sweet, slightly fortified wine

Vin jaune: sherry-like wine made in the Jura, eastern France.

ITALIAN LABELS

Italy's wine labels are some of the most emphatically "designed" and "artistic" in the world, as the examples elsewhere in this book prove. This occasionally means that labelling laws which are supposed to apply to all winemaking countries of the EEC are set aside in the interests of producing an eye-catching bottle. However, the following are the terms which should feature on Italian bottles.

One word of warning: look out for *vino da tàvola*, meaning literally "table wine". It covers both the very cheapest and nastiest of Italy's wines, and some of the most expensive and best. Sadly, the inadequacies of the Italian legal appellation system has encouraged enterprising winemakers to opt out and to sell wine under their own name, rather than with a regional designation.

Alto Adige: wine region, also Sud Tirol

Amabile: semi-sweet

Amaro: bitter

Annata: vintage

Asti: wine region

Azienda: estate

Barabaresco: red wine

Barbera: red wine and grape

Bardolino: red wine

Barolo: red wine

Bianco: white

Brunello: black grape and wine

Brunello di montalcino: red wine

Cabernet: black grape and wine

Cantina: winery

Carmignano: red wine

Casa vinicola: wine producer — usually merchant

Charmat: sparkling wine made by the tank method, producing less high quality wine

Chiaretto: pale red/rosé

Classico: theoretically the best, traditional vineyards within a region — eg Chianti Classico

Colle/colli: hill/s

Consorzio: consortium of growers — eg Chianti Putto

Corvo: Sicilian estate

DOC (Denominazione di Origine Controllata): Italy's less thorough equivalent of *Appellation Contrôlée*

DOCG (Denominazione di Origine Controllata e Garantita): stricter version of DOC, operating in a limited number of regions

Dolce: sweet

Dolcetto: dry red wine

Fattoria: estate

Fermentazione naturale: *cuve close*, sparkling wine

Frascati: white wine

Frizzante: sparkling

Galestro: white wine

Gavi: white wine

Imbotiglato nel'origine: estate bottled

Lambrusco: sparkling red and white wine

Liquoroso: strong, usually sweet, wine

Malvasia: grape variety

Marsala: sweet, fortified, Sicilian wine

Montepulciano: red wine and grape of the same name

Moscato: sweet fizzy wine

Nebbiolo: black grape

Nero: red

Orvieto: white wine

Passito: sweet, raisiny wine made from dried grapes

Piedmont: wine region

Podere: estate

Putto: Chianti consortium

Recioto: dry-sweet, raisiny wine

Riserva: wine which has spent a specified length of time in a barrel

Riserva speciale: as above, but aged for longer

Rosato: rosé

Rosso: red

Secco: dry

Semisecco: semi-dry

Spumante: sparkling

Stravecchio: extra old

Sud Tirol: north-east wine region

Superiore: usually wine which has undergone prolonged ageing

Tenementi: estate

Tenuta: estate

Vecchio: estate

Vendemmia: vintage

VIDE: group of quality-conscious producers

Vigna: vineyard

Vigneto: vineyard

Vino da pasto: basic table wine

Vino novello: wine sold within months of the harvest

Vino da tàvola: literally "table wine", but including some of Italy's very best

Vin santo: sweet wine made from dried grapes

Vitigno: grape variety

SPANISH LABELS

Spanish labels are much more informative than they used to be.

Until very recently, for example, bottles on show in Spanish shops bore no vintage information, apart from the fact that a wine was a second, third or fourth *año*, which indicated the number of years it had spent in the barrel before bottling. Since there was no way of knowing how long the bottle might have been in the shop, the wine's age remained a mystery — as did the quality of the vintage.

When vintage labels did appear, they were often of little use, since there was a tradition of choosing numbers at random and even, in at least one case, of using a telephone number rather than the genuine year of production. Nowadays, thankfully, the information is more reliable.

Abocado: medium sweet

Almacenista: old, unblended sherry

Amontillado: aged Fino sherry, usually medium dry — literally means 'made like Montilla'

Amoroso: sweet Oloroso

Alella: wine region

Añada: sherry of a single year (rare)

Año: year, often as in second or third year — the one in which the wine is bottled after cask ageing

Blanco: white

Bodega: winery

Cariñena: confusingly, both the name of a region and of a grape which does not produce most of that region's wine

Cava: champagne-method fizzy wine

Clarete: paler red wine

Con crianza: oak-aged — used to denote reasonable Rioja

Cosecha: vintage

DO (Denominación de Origen): Spain's *appellation* system

Dulce: sweet

Dulce color: sweet, dark Malaga

Elaborado por: matured and bottled by

Embotellado por: bottled by

Espumoso: sparkling

Fino: pale, dry, delicate sherry

Generoso: dessert, fortified, sweet wine

Gran reserva: in Rioja, red wine which is at least seven years old with at least four years in barrel, or eight years in bottle. With white wines, the minimum ageing is four years, of which at least six months has to have been in barrel. Outside Rioja, red *gran reserva* will have spent at least two years in barrel, three in bottle.

Gran vas: *cuve close* fizzy wine

Jerez: the only legal source for wine labelled "sherry"

Jumilla: wine region

Lagrime: finest quality Malaga

Malaga: sweet dessert wine

Manzanilla: salty, fino-like wine, made on the coast near Jerez

Montilla: sherry-like, but unfortified wine from Montilla

Navarra: wine region

Oloroso: full-bodied — dry or sweet — sherry

Pajarete: dry or medium dry Malaga

Palo cortado: sherry which is a cross between Fino and Oloroso (rare)

Pasado, pasada: good old Amontillado and Fino

Penedés: wine region

Raya: lesser quality Oloroso

Reserva: red Rioja which is at least five years old, with two and half years in cask; white Rioja, at least six months' cask ageing. Red *reservas* from other regions must have had three years' ageing, one in cask; for white wines, three years ageing, two in cask

Rioja (Alta, Alavesa, Baja): wine region, and its sub-regions

Rosado: rosé

Seco: dry

Semi-seco: semi-dry

Sin crianza: non-aged

Tinto: red

Valdepeñas: wine region

Vendimia: vintage

PORTUGUESE LABELS

Although Portugal has a long-established system of regional appellations, it also has a long tradition of producing first class wines which have no place within that system at all. So while Portuguese wine drinkers might request specifically a *Douro* or a *Bairrada*, they are often happy simply to choose between a *Vinho Verde* (a young wine, red or white) and a *Vinho Maduro* (an older wine). The fact that *Vinho Verde* is also the name of a very extensive demarcated region and that old bottles of this "drink-young-at-all-costs" wine are all too often found in Portugal is unfortunate. Equally frustrating is the way in which individual producers can designate their wine *garrafeira* or *reserva* more or less as they please

Port producers are, in theory, strictly controlled in the way in which they label their wine. However, the incidence of such meaningless terms as "very special", "finest", and "superior" does little to help the wine buyer, although there are plans to tighten up port-labelling practices.

Adega: winery
Alvarinho: white grape variety
Bairrada: red and white wine region
Branco: white
Bual: sweet Madeira — not quite as sweet as Malmsey
Colheita: vintage *Colheita* port (unavailable in Britain) is a tawny port of a single vintage. To most people this is a contradiction in terms, as the best tawny is always a blend of several vintages
Crusted, crusting: port of one or more vintages which has been bottled young, so needs decanting
Dão: red and white wine region
Douro: red and white wine region
Dulce: sweet
Engarrafado: bottled by
Espumante: sparkling
Garrafeira: of a particularly high quality — as determined by the producer, rather than by law
Generoso: strong, sweet
LBV (late bottled vintage): port bottled between four to six years after the harvest — can be similar to vintage or ruby
Madeira: fortified wine from the island of the same name
Malmsey: very sweet Madeira
Quinta: farm, estate
Rainwater: dryish Madeira
Região demarcada: designated region
Reserva: a producer's top quality wine
Rosado: rosé
Ruby: basic port
Seco: dry
Sercial: dry Madeira — not as dry as Verdelho
Tawny: port which has aged for 20 or more years in the barrel. Cheaper versions are blends of ruby and white
Tinto: red
Velho, velhas: old
Verdelho: very dry Madeira
Vinho consumo: basic table wine
Vinho doce: sweet wine
Vinho maduro: mature wine
Vinho verde: young red and white wine from the region Vinhos Verdes
Vintage character: better quality ruby
Vintage port: port of a declared year which has matured in bottle (rare)

GERMAN LABELS

The first problem with German wine labels is managing to read what they say; on occasion, even a Berliner might find the ornate gothic script just a little hard to decipher.

The next task is to decide which part of the word-covered label is really important. Certain vineyards do traditionally make the best wine, as do certain producers, but the ungenerous German climate makes even these indications less reliable than they might be in wines made in a warmer climate.

Of crucial importance are the quality and sweetness level (the best wines all being labelled QmP rather than the very ordinary QbA and range in sweetness from *Kabinett* to *Trockenbeerenauslese*), and the grape variety.

Ahr: wine region

Abfüllung: bottling (as in bottled by)

AP (amtliche prüfungsnummer): identifying code number on every bottle of wine sold

Auslese: late harvest — sweeter than Spätlese, less sweet than Beerenauslese

Baden: wine region

Bereich: specified, though often undistinguished wine region — eg Bereich Nierstein

Burg: castle

Deutscher sekt: *cuve close* (often poor) fizzy wine which until recently was legally made from imported wine, despite its name

Deutscher Tafelwein: German basic table wine — as opposed to blended EEC *tafelwein*

Diabetiker wein: very dry wine — for diabetics

Eiswein: very concentrated, rare, sweet wine made from grapes picked while frozen

Erben: "heirs" — usually part of a producer's name

Erzeugenabfullung: estate-bottled

Franken: wine region

Halbtrocken: almost dry

Hessiche Bergstrasse: small wine region

Hock: wine from the Rhine

Kabinett: driest, higher quality wine

Landwein: basic dry wine

Liebfraumilch: usually basic sweet wine from the Rhine, rarely seen in Germany

Mittelrhein: wine region

Mösel-Saar-Ruwer: wine region

Morio-muskat: grape variety

Müller-Thurgau: grape variety

Nahe: wine region

Originalabfüllung: estate-bottled

Perlwein: slightly sparkling

Prädikatsweinguter weingut: quality wine estate

QbA (Qualitätswein bestimmter Anbaugebieter): so-called "quality wine" from one of 11 specified regions invariably sweetened with unfermented grape juice. Some of Germany's poorest wine, including all Liebfraumilch, is QbA

QmP (Qualitätswein mit Prädikat): Genuinely quality wine — no added sweetening is allowed

Rheingau: wine region

Rheinhessen: wine region

Rheinpfalz: wine region

Riesling: Germany's finest grape variety

Rötling: light red wine made from black and white grapes

Rotwein: red wine

Schaumwein: sparkling wine, more basic than *sekt*

Schillerwein: Rotwein from Würtemberg

Schloss: castle

Sekt: *cuve close* sparkling wine

Spätlese: medium sweet (usually), late picked wine always of QmP standard

Trocken: dry

Trockenbeerenauslese: very, very late picked; extremely sweet

Verband Deutscher: quality wine consortium

Weingut: wine estate — only legally used on wine made from the estate's own grapes

Weissherbst: rosé made from a single grape variety

Winzergenossenschaft: cooperative

Winzerverein: cooperative

Würtemberg: wine region

Zentralkellerei: enormous central cellar uniting a group of cooperatives

AUSTRALIAN LABELS

As in the US, Australian wine labelling law is very relaxed when it comes to calling a wine "claret", "Burgundy" or "port". Only champagne is more strictly controlled as it is required to be made either in the same way as champagne, or by the similar, but less good, "transfer method".

Unlike the US, however, wines misleadingly labelled with European names can be among the best in the country, if not expected to taste anything like their European counterparts. In more than one instance, the same wine at Australian wine fairs has won gold medals in both the "claret" and "Burgundy" classes.

There has been a move, however, towards varietal labelling, with Chardonnay and Cabernet Sauvignon, for example, featuring more often than ever before. Look out for unusual marriages of grape varieties; the Australians have proven very adept at blending varieties grown in the Rhône with ones grown in Bordeaux and producing really great and individual wines in the process.

Bin: many Australian wines are known by "bin numbers" such as 111 or 999 — there seems little logic to the choice of numbers

Champagne: sparkling wine made by *Méthode Champenoise* or by the transfer method

Coonawarra: one of the most

up-and-coming wine regions — particularly for red wine

Hermitage: Shiraz (q.v.), but can be a blend

Hunter Valley Riesling: Semillon grape variety

Rhine Riesling: the Riesling

grape variety as distinct from Hunter Valley Riesling

Shiraz: Syrah grape variety, used to make Hermitage in France

AMERICAN LABELS

North American wine labels are divided into three groups: generic, varietal and proprietory. The first group shamelessly use terms such as "port", "sherry", "champagne", "Burgundy", "Chianti" and "Chablis" to describe wines which have not even the faintest family resemblance to the European wines to which they refer. Varietal labels, by contrast, are more honest, stating the grape variety or varieties from which a wine has been made. Proprietory labels feature quite strongly, with names such as *Petite Rosé* appearing on wines of varying styles.

Outside California, the range of grape varieties used becomes even wider and includes names such as the Baco, Delaware and Catawba which are almost exclusive to North America. Perhaps best known, though far from best, of these is the Concord, a grape which makes very good jelly. The honesty of these labels, however, is less than absolute because, for example, since only 75% of a wine labelled "Cabernet Sauvignon" has to be made from that grape; before 1983, the figure was even lower.

Blanc de Noirs: rosé

Blush: rosé by any other name

Concord: grape variety used to make good grape jelly and very poor wine

Gamay Beaujolais: a type of Pinôt Noir, not the Gamay grown in the Beaujolais

Grey Riesling: a grape unrelated to the Riesling

Johannisberg Riesling: uses the genuine Riesling grape

Late Harvest: California's answer to Auslese

Light wines: wines with low alcohol levels

Petite Sirah: a grape unrelated to the Syrah of the Rhône

Private Reserve: a meaningless term used by wineries

Proprietor's Selection: a meaningless term used by wineries

Reserve: a meaningless term used by wineries

Riesling: quite probably the less distinguished Sylvaner whose wines can call themselves Riesling. More honest labellers call such wine "Riesling-

Sylvaner" or "Franken-Riesling". Genuine Riesling is called Johannisberg Riesling

Ruby Cabernet: Californian cross between Cabernet and Carignane (a variety the French know as Carignan). Other such crosses include the Carmine, Centurion and Carnelian

Select Late Harvest: California's answer to Beerenauslese

Special Select Late Harvest: California's answer to Trockenbeerenauslese

Special Selection: a meaningless term used by wineries

Vinifera: wine grapes, rather than Labrusca which, though used for wine, are eating grapes, and hybrids, which are a cross between the two

White: either white wine, or, as in "White Zinfandel", pink

Wine coolers: mixtures of wine, water, fruit juice, soda and artificial flavouring — tasting most of the latter

TYPICAL
LABELS

WINE EXPERTS OFTEN FIND THEMSELVES FACED WITH ANONYMOUS GLASSES OF WINE TO IDENTIFY, AND FEW PEOPLE COULD HONESTLY CLAIM NEVER TO HAVE STOLEN A PEEK AT THE BOTTLE. WITH LUCK, IT CAN BE POSSIBLE TO SPOT THAT THE BOTTLE WITH THE SLOPING SHOULDERS HAS A RHONE-STYLE LABEL RATHER THAN A BURGUNDY ONE. BUT WITH BORDEAUX, IT CAN BE A LITTLE MORE DIFFICULT; AFTER ALL, THERE ARE ALL THOSE NON-BORDEAUX BOTTLES WITH CHATEAUX ON THEIR LABELS.

WHILE THERE IS AN INCREASING TREND TOWARDS INDIVIDUALITY IN THE CHOICE OF LABELS, THE SELECTION PROCESS IS OFTEN LIMITED TO A VISIT TO THE LOCAL PRINTER. A TRADITIONAL PRINTER MAY HAVE A FILE FULL OF BASIC WINE LABEL DESIGNS, JUST AS HE HAS A SELECTION OF STYLES OF WEDDING INVITATIONS. ALL A GROWER HAS TO DO IS CHOOSE THE STYLE HE LIKES BEST, GIVE THE PRINTER THE NAMES OF THE WINES PRODUCED (EACH BURGUNDIAN GROWER, FOR EXAMPLE, WILL TEND TO MAKE WINES OF AT LEAST FOUR OR FIVE DIFFERENT APPELLATIONS), AND A BATCH OF LABELS CAN BE MADE UP.

F R A N C E

ALTHOUGH THERE HAS BEEN A RECENT GROWTH OF "DESIGNER LABELS" IN FRANCE, THE WINES OF ITS PRINCIPAL WINE-PRODUCING REGIONS ARE STILL LABELLED IN STYLES WHICH WOULD HAVE BEEN RECOGNIZABLE A CENTURY AGO. EVEN THEN ONE REGION'S WINES WERE DISTINGUISHED FROM THOSE OF ANOTHER.

RED WINES FROM THE LOIRE AND BOTH RED AND WHITE WINES FROM BURGUNDY OFTEN HAVE "PARCHMENTY" LABELS, WHICH SEEM TO HAVE BEEN DEVISED TO GIVE THEM A MEDIEVAL FLAVOUR. THE RHONE ACHIEVES A SIMILAR EFFECT WITH ITS ORNATE GOTHIC SCRIPT, SEEN TO BEST EFFECT ON THE CHATEAUNEUF DU PAPE LABEL WHICH ALSO INCLUDES THE INEVITABLE PAPAL MITRE AND KEYS.

BORDEAUX IS OFTEN THOUGHT TO HAVE THE MONOPOLY IN "CHATEAU" LABELS BUT THE STYLE HAS BEEN ADOPTED BY OTHER REGIONS THROUGHOUT SOUTHERN FRANCE. MISTAKES CAN EASILY BE MADE BETWEEN WINES OF DIFFERENT REGIONS, AND ONLY THE SMALLER PRINT OF THE APPELLATION AND GROWER'S ADDRESS WILL CONFIRM WHICH IS WHICH.

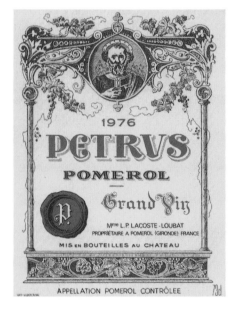

The name Beychevelle derives from the French for "drop your sail", a practice adopted by ships passing the Port de Beychevelle close to the château. Château Petrus is, arguably, the greatest red wine in the world and, unarguably, the most expensive. Being in Pomerol, rather than the Médoc or St. Emilion, it is, however, not classed as a <u>grand cru</u>. Château Figeac retains an old-fashioned air and Château d'Yquem uses a very plain classic label.

ABOVE: Burgundy favours overtly traditional labels, such as this one for Morgon. The Bourgogne Rouge "Tastevinage" label indicates that this wine has been tried by a panel of experts at an annual tasting. All wines which pass this tasting — red or white — carry this label on which the producer's name is less prominent. White Burgundy, such as this Chablis from the Montmains vineyard, often wears this kind of plain label. The Hermitage label refers to the fact that this Rhône comes from vines grown around a small chapel at the top of the Hermitage vineyard. OPPOSITE: The Beaune Bressandes is a <u>premier cru</u> which was bottled at the domaine, unusual for a Burgundy of this age.

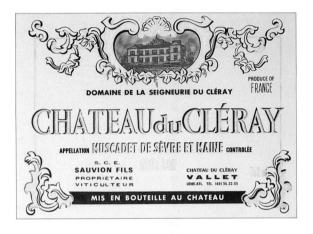

ABOVE: Loire labels tend to be fairly old-fashioned in their style. Alsace labels are recognisable by the Germanic names of both villages and producers. This particular example is a <u>grand cru</u> but, as usual in Alsace, it is the grape variety — in this case the Riesling — which is all-important. OPPOSITE: This Arbois label from eastern France is particularly old-fashioned in style.

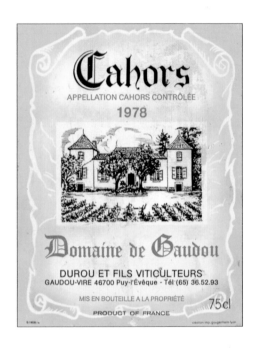

Champagne labels vary between the austerely plain, such as Pol Roger and
Krug, to the ornate Dom Perignon. Those who drink Pol Roger outside
Britain will notice an absence of the black border which appears only on
bottles exported to the UK. That funereal border is precisely what it seems:
an homage to Sir Winston Churchill, one of Pol Roger's most ardent fans.
From less exalted regions of France, the possibly phallic Côtes de Provence
label is very typical, and well suited to the peculiar shape of the region's
bottles. Cahors is an old-fashioned wine whose style is reflected in its labels;
Vin de Pays des Côtes de Gascogne, on the other hand, is a modern,
inexpensive country white wine.

ITALY

ITALY'S LABELS ARE SUCH A MIXED BAG OF DESIGN AND ART THAT IT IS INCREASINGLY DIFFICULT TO DISCERN REGIONAL STYLES. EVEN SO, PARTICULAR WINE REGIONS ARE RECOGNIZABLE; THE ALTO ADIGE — OR SUD TIROL AS IT IS ALSO KNOWN — OFTEN REFLECTS ITS AUSTRO-ITALIAN CHARACTER WITH LABELS THAT LOOK MORE GERMANIC THAN MANY FROM THE RHINE OR THE MOSEL.

IN TUSCANY, THERE IS A TASTE FOR RENAISSANCE FIGURES, COATS OF ARMS AND ILLUSTRATIONS OF THE REGION'S MANY CASTLES AND FARMS. VERDICCHIO LOOKS BACK TO THE DAYS OF ANCIENT WINEGROWING, WITH A GRECIAN—STYLE SCRIPT TO MATCH ITS AMPHORA-SHAPED BOTTLE, AND IN THE PIEDMONT, LABELS OF BARBARESCO AND BAROLO OFTEN SEEM TO MIRROR THE TOUGH, "OLD-FASHIONED" FLAVOURS OF THOSE WINES.

A classic Brunello di Montalcino label which makes use of medieval imagery and vibrant colours.

Wines from the north east of Italy often have apparently Germanic labels, such as the St. Magdelener label. The Bardolino label is more traditional in style, and surprisingly classy for a rosé. The Colli Orientali is another fresh young wine labelled in almost the same way as the producer's range of varietal wines. The Soave is from one of the region's best vineyards.

This Grignolino label is interesting for its use of traditional design and its inclusion of the VIDE device. Venegazzu, like the Sicilian Regaleali, is a top-quality table wine, but it is not made under the restrictions of a designated DOC or DOCG region. Masi, a very good producer, uses a very classic label for its Amarone, one of the most classic of Italian wines.

ABOVE: The Biondi-Santi family produce the most expensive, and possibly the best, Brunello di Montalcino. Pio Cesare is a good name to find on Barbaresco labels, as is Gaja, while Ferrari (unrelated to the motor manufacturer) make very good champagne-style fizzy wine. Incidentally, the car-producing Signor Lamborghini does makes sparkling wine under his own name. OPPOSITE: An apparently hand-written label on a bottle of Amarone.

SPAIN

DESPITE THE INTERNATIONAL SUCCESS OF RIOJA, SPAIN HAS BEEN THE SOURCE OF VERY LITTLE LABEL INNOVATION THE SPANISH CHARACTER IS APPARENT IN LABELS WHICH RELY HEAVILY ON THE SCRIPT IN WHICH THE WINE NAME IS PRINTED, THE PRESENCE OF MEDALS (USUALLY WON IN COMPETITIONS HELD A CENTURY AGO) AND IMPRESSIVE COATS OF ARMS. THIS LAST FEATURE IS PERHAPS NOT SURPRISING WHEN ONE CONSIDERS HOW MANY WINES INCLUDE THE NAME OF THE *MARQUES DE* THIS OR THAT IN THEIR TITLES. RIOJA BOTTLES ARE ALSO OFTEN RECOGNIZABLE BY THE GOLD "STRING BAGS" WHICH SURROUND THEM.

APART FROM RIOJA AND CAVA (THE SPARKLING WINES WITH THEIR OWN LABELLING STYLE WHICH OFTEN DELIBERATELY MIMICS THAT OF CHAMPAGNE), REGIONS SUCH AS NAVARRA AND VALDEPENAS ARE ONLY BEGINNING TO ACHIEVE INTERNATIONAL RECOGNITION. THEY TEND TO HAVE SIMILARLY OLD FASHIONED LABELS — BUT WITH FEWER MEDALS AND LESS HERALDRY.

A 40-year-old bottle of Rioja, complete with the stamp of authenticity.

ABOVE: The Torres family (note the three towers on the trademark) is the big name in the Penedés region; Gran Coronas is one of its successful red blends. The Marqués de Murrieta makes very traditional Rioja; this Castillo Ygay 1942 was only released recently onto the market. Logroño is the town in which the cellar is to be found. The Las Campana, despite the words "Elaboracion Especial", is a fairly basic white wine from Navarra, while the Ribeiro comes from a region by the border with Portugal. Compare this label with that of the Portuguese Douro on page 57. OPPOSITE: Faustino V is this company's name for its Reserva Rioja.

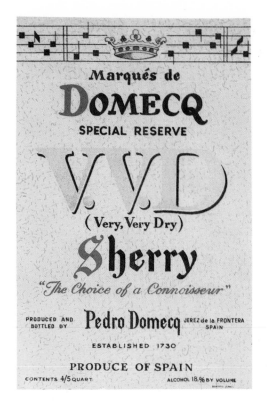

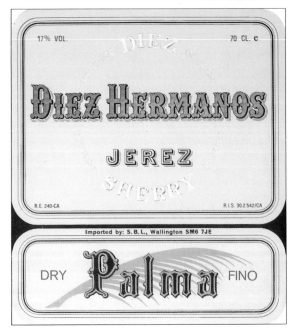

Harvey's Bristol Cream is probably the best known sweet sherry, and refers to the town through which it was shipped. The Diez Hermanos sherry is a Fino, so the word "dry" is theoretically unnecessary. Domecq, another great sherry house, emphasises the dry nature of this wine for the US market, while Domingo Perez Marin have produced a truly classic label for their dry sherry from Manzanilla, the seaside town near Jerez. The Sanchez Romate labels are very typical of styles used for both the Spanish and the export markets.

PORTUGAL

*M*ANY PEOPLE THINK OF PORTUGUESE WINE IN TERMS OF JUST ONE WINE — MATEUS ROSE — AND ITS INSTANTLY RECOGNIZABLE LABEL. NOT SURPRISINGLY, THE MATEUS DESIGN HAS BEEN COPIED BY THE PRODUCERS OF JUST ABOUT EVERY OTHER PORTUGUESE ROSE, AND PALACES OF ONE KIND OR ANOTHER SEEM TO FEATURE ON EVERY LABEL. IT IS ONLY WHEN ONE COMES TO THE MORE CLASSIC WINES, SUCH AS DAO, BAIRRADA AND DOURO, THAT A SPECIFICALLY "PORTUGUESE" STYLE BECOMES APPARENT, AND EVEN THEN THE SMALL NUMBER OF PRODUCERS AND MERCHANTS DISPLAY A RELATIVELY LACKLUSTRE SET OF LABELS WITH FEW EXCEPTIONS.

The Moscatel from Setubal is one of the world's great sweet wines, and the company of José Maria da Fonseca maintains a magnificent stock of casks of old wine, this one being 20 years old. The parchmenty Bairrada label, like that of the Douro, is very typical of traditional Portuguese labelling. Note the word "Garrafeira" indicating special selection by the producer. The Mateus label needs no explanation — except that the pretty bottle contains 700cl rather than the more usual 750cl.

ABOVE: Wood port — this one is from London's most traditional merchant — is another name for Tawny wine which has aged in barrel rather than bottle. Both Madeiras are from the same producer, with the ducal names and the words Malmsey and Bual indicating their individual styles. The original Mr. Blandy was the first person to commercialise Madeira internationally. Spratley's Late Bottle Vintage is a port which has been left in cask for over four years before bottling (this 1967 was bottled in 1973). OPPOSITE: The Hutchesons, by contrast, is a true vintage port, matured in bottle.

GERMANY

CONSIDERING THAT GERMANY WAS ONE OF THE FIRST COUNTRIES TO PRINT WINE LABELS — ONES OF ENDURING BEAUTY — IT IS SURPRISING HOW LITTLE INNOVATION THERE HAS BEEN IN GERMAN LABEL DESIGN OVER THE LAST CENTURY. THIS MAY BE DUE TO THE MASS OF INFORMATION WHICH HAS TO FEATURE ON A GERMAN LABEL (WINE NAME, QUALITY LEVEL, GRAPE VARIETY, REGION OF PRODUCTION). WHATEVER THE EXPLANATION, THERE ARE THREE BASIC ELEMENTS IN THEIR DESIGN. SOME HAVE COATS OF ARMS, SOME HAVE VIEWS OF VINEYARDS WHEREAS OTHERS MAKE DO WITH ORNATE SCRIPT. OTHERS AGAIN INVOLVE TWO OR MORE OF THESE ELEMENTS. HOWEVER, APART FROM THE LABELS OF A SELECT FEW ESTATES, IT IS ONLY THE USUALLY ARCH-BACKED CAT FEATURED ON ZELLER SCHWARZE KATZ AND THE ROUNDED LABELS ON THE FLASK-SHAPED FRANCONIAN WINE BOTTLES WHICH REALLY STAND OUT.

WATCH OUT FOR LABELS WHICH SAY *TROCKEN* OR *HALB-TROCKEN*. THESE INDICATE RESPECTIVELY DRY, AND DRIER THAN USUAL, WINES. WATCH OUT TOO FOR *CHARTA* LABELS, INDICATING MEMBERSHIP OF A QUALITY-CONSCIOUS GROUP OF PRODUCERS.

This label is from the Scharzhofberg vineyard, and was made by Egon Müller, owner of the Scharzhof house at the foot of the vineyard and of the best estate in the Saar region. 1970 was not a great vintage, hence no mention of Kabinett, Spätlese or Auslese.

RHEINGAU · Erbach

1982 Bereich Johannisberg

Riesling - Qualitätswein

Erzeuger-Abfüllung · A. P. Nr. 32 091 019 83 e 70 cl

Bottled by: Produce of Germany

WINZERGENOSSENSCHAFT ERBACH eG

ERBACH IM RHEINGAU

· MOSEL · SAAR · RUWER ·

70 cl **1985er**

Graacher Himmelreich
Riesling - Kabinett

Qualitätswein mit Prädikat — Erzeuger-Abfüllung

A. P. Nr. 2 576 280 081 86
Produced and bottled in Germany

ZENTRALKELLEREI MOSEL-SAAR-RUWER; BERNKASTEL-KUES

Produce of Germany

Mitglied im Verband
Deutscher Qualitäts- und Prädikatsweingüter

Wein Reichsrat v. Buhl · Rhein Deidesheim

Rheinpfalz – Qualitätswein mit Prädikat

1983er Forster Ungeheuer
Riesling Spätlese

e 0,75 l ERZEUGERABFÜLLUNG Amtl. Prüf.-Nr. 5 106 044 27 84

WEINGUT REICHSRAT VON BUHL DEIDESHEIM/WEINSTRASSE 8327

1977er
Qualitätswein

A. P. Nr.
40188 002 78

e 0,7 L

ERBACH RHEINGAU

Schloss Reinhartshausen

A. P. Nr. 32 071 030 77

1976er Hattenheimer Nußbrunnen Riesling

Qualitätswein mit Prädikat Auslese

SCHLOSS REINHARTSHAUSEN · 6229 ERBACH

Hochheimer
KÖNIGIN VICTORIA BERG
RHEINGAU RIESLING
Erzeugerabfüllung
G. M. PABSTMANN SOHN
Alleiniger Eigenthümer
HOCHHEIM A/MAIN

The Bereich Johannisberg gave the Riesling in the US its name of Johannisberg Riesling. Von Buhl is one of the best producers in the Rheinpfalz; this is a Spätlese. Schloss Reinhartshausen's classic label is for a late-picked Riesling from the Hattenheimer Nussbrunnen vineyard. The Graacher Himmelreich is a top-quality wine from the Mosel. The Konigin Victoria Berg, despite its ornate label, is only a basic QbA. This is because it was produced in the unripe 1977 vineyard. In a better year, it deserves its reputation as Queen Victoria's favourite. The Dr. Burklin-Wolf wine is a dry rosé made from the same grape — the "Spätburgunder" — as red Burgundy. "Cabinet" on the 1921 Steinberger, a very sweet Trockenbeerenauslese, indicates a wine of particularly high quality. It should not be confused with Kabinett, which would indicate a far drier wine. Present-day labels from this estate are almost unchanged. Naturrein was the old expression for QmP.

SWITZERLAND & AUSTRIA

SWISS WINE LABELLING CAN BE VERY CONFUSING BECAUSE WINES ARE NAMED BOTH AFTER GRAPE VARIETIES AND PLACES. FOR EXAMPLE, FENDANT IS A GRAPE (KNOWN IN FRANCE AS CHASSELAS) AND DOLE IS BOTH A PLACE AND A WINE MADE FROM THE PINOT NOIR. IN ADDITION, NORTH AND EAST SWITZERLAND HAVE DIFFERENT RULES TO WEST SWITZERLAND. BEWARE, TOO, CONFUSING THE ERMITAGE (THE FRENCH MARSANNE GRAPE) WITH HERMITAGE FROM AUSTRALIA AND SOUTH AFRICA — OR HERMITAGE ITSELF AND THE JOHANNISBERG (THE SWISS NAME FOR THE SYLVANER) WITH JOHANNISBERG RIESLING.

AS EXPECTED WITH THE VARIED NATIONALITIES OF THE SWISS, LABELS VARY IN STYLE ENORMOUSLY DEPENDING ON THE FRENCH, ITALIAN OR GERMAN HERITAGE OF EACH INDIVIDUAL PRODUCER, AND CAN BE VERY ATTRACTIVE. WINES WHICH ARE NOT DRY ARE LABELLED *LEGEREMENT DOUX* OR *AVEC SUCRE RESIDUEL*. MANY SWISS WINES ARE GIVEN BRANDNAMES, FOR EXAMPLE JOHANNISBERG RHEINGOLD, WHICH GIVE NO INDICATION OF QUALITY OR PROVENANCE.

ALTHOUGH AUSTRIAN LABELS CAN BE SIMILAR IN STYLE TO THOSE OF GERMANY, THEY ARE PERHAPS LESS ORNATE AND CLOSER TO A FRENCH STYLE, WITH ONLY THE SCRIPT REVEALING A MORE NORDIC INFLUENCE.

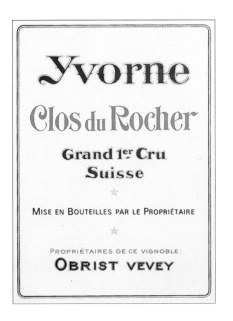

The Clos du Rocher is a <u>premier cru</u> and is thus an estate bottled wine. The Fechy, as a "dorin", will be made from the Chasselas grape. The Austrian Gewürztraminer is made by a very good producer but is evidently not of a good enough year to climb beyond Qualitätswein status. The Weissburgunder, by contrast, is a Kabinett made from the Pinot Blanc.

ENGLAND

ANYBODY WHO WANTED TO ILLUSTRATE THE NATURE OF THE FLEDGLING ENGLISH WINE INDUSTRY NEED DO NO MORE THAN DISPLAY A FEW LABELS. THERE IS AN ESSENTIALLY HOMESPUN STYLE TO MANY OF THEM, REVEALING THE "COTTAGE INDUSTRY" NATURE WHICH STILL BEDEVILS ENGLISH WINE PRODUCTION.

REGIONAL VARIATIONS IN STYLE ARE ONLY JUST BECOMING APPARENT. MOST WINES ARE SOLD UNDER THE NAME OF THE WINERY OR ESTATE WHICH PRODUCED THEM AS A "DRY" OR "MEDIUM DRY" WINE, OR, MORE FREQUENTLY, AS VARIETALS. THE NAMES OF ALL KINDS OF PREVIOUSLY UNHEARD-OF GERMANIC GRAPE VARIETIES, SUCH AS THE REICHENSTEINER, OPTIMA AND BACCHUS (AS WELL AS THE MORE FREQUENTLY ENCOUNTERED MULLER-THURGAU), ALONG WITH A SKETCH OF A THATCHED COTTAGE ARE USUALLY THE MARK OF AN ENGLISH WINE. GOLD, ROUND E.V.A. STICKERS INDICATE THAT A WINE HAS BEEN APPROVED BY THE ENGLISH VINEYARD ASSOCIATION.

BEWARE "BRITISH WINE" WHICH IS MADE FROM IMPORTED GRAPE JUICE CONCENTRATE AND HAS NOTHING WHATSOEVER TO DO WITH ENGLISH GRAPE GROWING OR WINEMAKING.

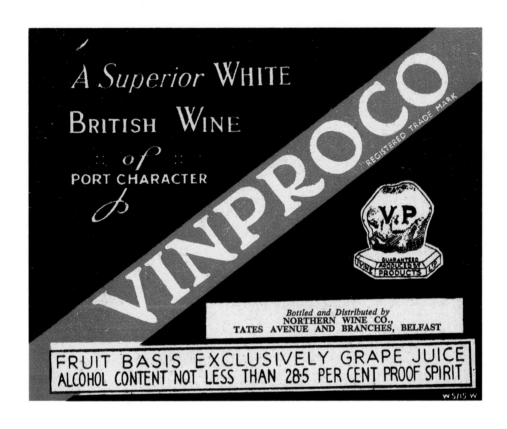

Warning! This is not, as one might think, a wine made from grapes grown in England. Like all "British" wine, "sherry" or "port", this is produced from concentrated grape juice imported from Cyprus or just about anywhere else.

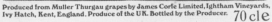

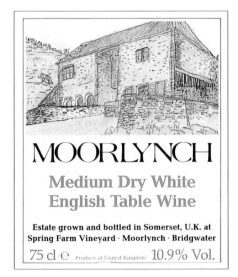

ABOVE: *Ightham and Moorlynch merely call themselves English table wine, although closer examination reveals the Ightham to be a Müller-Thurgau. Lamberhurst and Carr Taylor are two of Britain's most successful vineyards, both specialising in varietals like this Lamberhurst Huxelrebe. Carr Taylor is, however, unique in making a high quality English sparkling wine. It is actually a méthode champenoise, but due to impending EEC legislation, the label makes no mention of this.* OPPOSITE: *One of the most attractive of English labels, Breaky Bottom's, is also one of the most typical.*

UNITED STATES

*L*ABELS IN THE UNITED STATES ARE AS VARIED AS ITS WINES. ON THE ONE HAND, THERE IS THE PURLOINING OF EUROPEAN NAMES SUCH AS "BURGUNDY" AND "CHABLIS" TO DESCRIBE WINES WHICH ARE NO MORE SIMILAR TO THESE THAN THEY ARE TO COCA COLA; AND ON THE OTHER, THERE ARE THE WELL-DESIGNED ESTATE LABELS ADOPTED BY THE EVER GROWING NUMBER OF "BOUTIQUE" WINERIES.

GIVEN THIS DIVERSITY, IT IS DIFFICULT TO DISCERN AN OVERALL STYLE, NOR EVEN ONE WHICH UNITES PRODUCERS IN ONE REGION RATHER THAN ANOTHER; ONLY VERY CAREFUL EXAMINATION OF A LABEL WILL REVEAL THAT THE ST. HILARY VINEYARD IS IN CONNECTICUT WHILE THE ST. CLEMENT VINEYARD IS IN CALIFORNIA.

THE ONE TREND WHICH IS APPARENT THROUGHOUT THE UNITED STATES, HOWEVER, HAS BEEN A MOVE TOWARDS JUST THIS KIND OF LOCALISED LABELLING, WITH NAMES LIKE "RUSSIAN RIVER" AND "FINGER LAKES" FIGURING EVER LARGER ON LABELS.

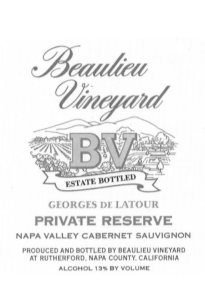

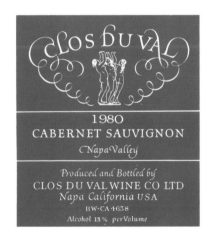

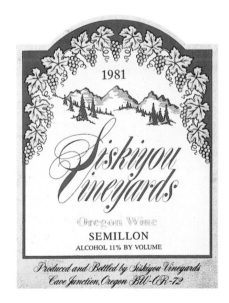

Known as BV, the Beaulieu vineyard produces excellent Cabernet Sauvignon in the Napa Valley. Domaine Chandon, owned by Moët & Chandon, carefully avoids calling its sparkling wine champagne. This wine, as a Blanc de Noirs, is a white wine made exclusively from black grapes. Clos du Val, also in the Napa Valley, has a French winemaker, the son of a winemaker at Château Lafite. Siskiyou Vineyards' label emphasises the cooler climate enjoyed by the vineyards of Oregon. Semillon is a fairly unusual variety here.

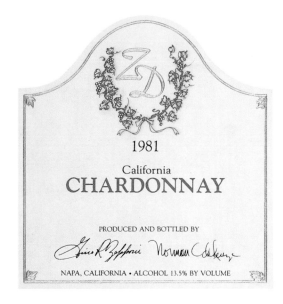

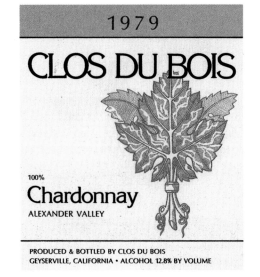

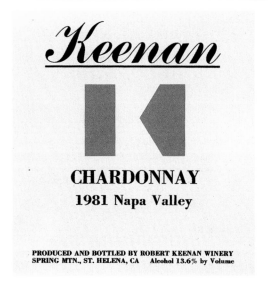

Steep, rocky vineyards and the cool, coastal climate (Region 1) of Western Sonoma County give Iron Horse Chardonnays their consistent and austere style: aromatic in the nose, supple in body, crisp, almost flinty in the finish. Small barrel fermentation makes this wine both subtle and complex with rich texture and great finesse. Bottle bouquet will intensify with extended bottle age.

1983
Sonoma County-Green Valley
Chardonnay

The grapes for this 100% Chardonnay wine were hand picked the 1st week of October. After 12 hours skin contact, half the wine was fermented in small French oak barrels, and half in French and Yugoslavian oak upright tanks. The lots were kept separate and aged 4 months in French oak barrels. Six lots were selected and blended in June; blend #1 of 4300 cases was bottled in July, 1984.

GROWN, PRODUCED & BOTTLED BY IRON HORSE VINEYARDS
SEBASTOPOL, CALIFORNIA, USA • ALCOHOL 12.2% BY VOLUME

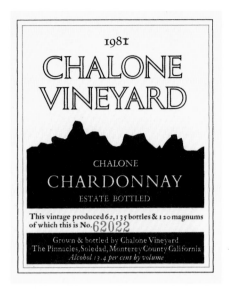

1981
CHALONE VINEYARD

CHALONE
CHARDONNAY
ESTATE BOTTLED

This vintage produced 62,135 bottles & 120 magnums of which this is No. 62022

Grown & bottled by Chalone Vineyard
The Pinnacles, Soledad, Monterey County California
Alcohol 13.4 per cent by volume

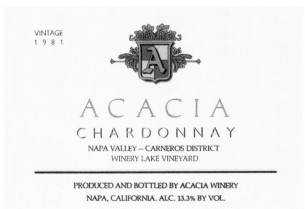

VINTAGE
1981

ACACIA
CHARDONNAY

NAPA VALLEY – CARNEROS DISTRICT
WINERY LAKE VINEYARD

PRODUCED AND BOTTLED BY ACACIA WINERY
NAPA, CALIFORNIA. ALC. 13.3% BY VOL.

SPECIAL SELECTION

Buena Vista

HARASZTHY CELLARS FOUNDED 1857
SONOMA VALLEY

Chardonnay

ESTATE GROWN AND BOTTLED BY
BUENA VISTA WINERY, CARNEROS, SONOMA, CALIFORNIA, USA
Alcohol 14.2% by Volume

Eight Californian Chardonnays show the range of label designs to be found in the US. Innisfree seems to have achieved an oriental rather than a Celtic feel to its label. Clos du Bois' label seems almost to look back to the Roman Empire, while ZD (Zero Defect), Keenan and Acacia all favour simplicity. The Iron Horse label is a particularly unusual shape. Note the presence of vineyard and regional names on these labels, and the fact that two of the wines are from Sonoma rather than the Napa Valley. The ZD is a "California" rather than a specifically regional wine. The Chalone from Monterey is one of the great California Chardonnays; the Buena Vista is from a winery named after Harazthy, father of Californian winemaking.

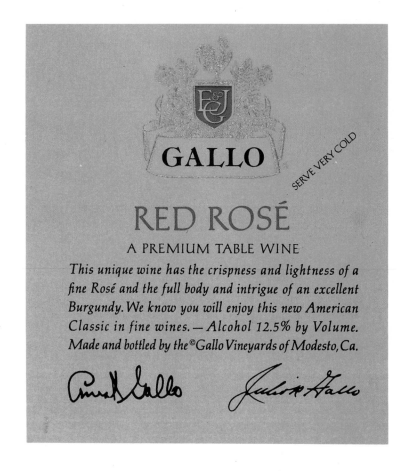

GALLO

SERVE VERY COLD

RED ROSÉ

A PREMIUM TABLE WINE

This unique wine has the crispness and lightness of a
fine Rosé and the full body and intrigue of an excellent
Burgundy. We know you will enjoy this new American
Classic in fine wines. — Alcohol 12.5% by Volume.
Made and bottled by the ©Gallo Vineyards of Modesto, Ca.

ABOVE: The Gallo winery is the biggest in the US and, as the signatures shown
here indicate, is still very much a family concern. *OPPOSITE:* Hamilton &
Tuttle's blush — or rosé — is from a firm of merchants who buy in and
blend wine, rather than from a winery. The floral label is intended to attract
female purchasers, as one of the firm's female directors admits.

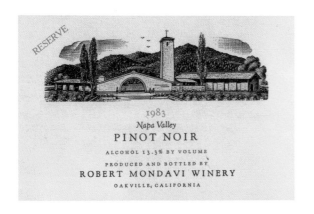

Robert Mondavi's graceful label shows his winery; the "Reserve" indicates a wine which should be better than the standard Pinot Noir. Monticello's Merlot is not to be confused with the California winery of the same name. Amity Vineyard's Oregon Pinot Noir, Missouri's The Abbey and Fred's Friends have styles all of their own.

AUSTRALIA

WHEN LOOKING AT MANY OF THE LABELS FROM AUSTRALIA'S MORE RECENTLY ESTABLISHED WINERIES, IT IS DIFFICULT TO TELL THEM APART FROM WINES PRODUCED IN THE NAPA VALLEY, CALIFORNIA OR NEW ZEALAND. THE LONGER-ESTABLISHED FIRMS, HOWEVER, SEEM FOND OF TOTALLY MEANINGLESS "BIN NUMBERS" — TRADITIONALLY, WINES WERE OFTEN KNOWN SIMPLY AS BIN 111 OR 999, RATHER THAN BY THEIR GRAPE VARIETY OR PROVENANCE. THEY ALSO INCLUDE LISTINGS OF ALL OF THE MEDALS AND TROPHIES WON AT THE ALL-IMPORTANT REGIONAL WINE SHOWS.

REGIONAL DESIGNATIONS ARE BECOMING INCREASINGLY IMPORTANT AND INCLUDE AREAS SUCH AS COONAWARRA, HUNTER VALLEY AND BAROSSA.

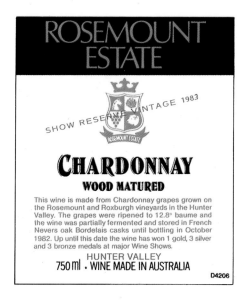

The blending of Cabernet Sauvignon and Shiraz is typically Australian. Penfold's is one of the biggest firms in Australia, and Murray Tyrrell pioneered Chardonnay growing in the Hunter Valley although Pinot Chardonnay is misleading — experts agree that the Chardonnay and Pinot grapes are unrelated. Rosemount's Show Reserve Chardonnay, like most of Australia's top wines, has been matured in new oak barrels.

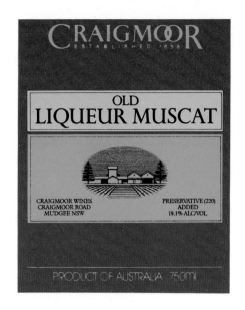

ABOVE: More traditional are labels from Yellowglen who, thanks to the French roots of the winemaker, term their wine <u>méthode champenoise</u> rather than champagne. Craigmoor's Liqueur Muscat label respects new laws by stating that it contains a preservative. Brown Brothers is one of the best producers in the State of Victoria and Berri Estates is a large cooperative. *OPPOSITE:* Using fabric labels is unusual even in Australia.

NEW ZEALAND

THE NEW ZEALAND WINE INDUSTRY IS SO YOUNG — A LARGE PROPORTION OF IT DATING FROM THE 1960S AND 1970S — THAT IT HAS NOT REALLY HAD TIME TO EVOLVE ITS OWN LABEL STYLE. ESSENTIALLY, AS IN AUSTRALIA AND THE UNITED STATES, WINES ARE SOLD AS VARIETALS, AND UNDER THE NAME OF THE MAJOR WINERY OR ESTATE WHICH PRODUCED THEM. THE MOST WIDELY PLANTED GRAPE IS THE MULLER-THURGAU (THE VARIETY USED IN BOTH GERMANY AND ENGLAND FOR ITS EARLY-RIPENING QUALITIES).

IT IS TRADITIONALLY KNOWN HERE AS THE RIESLING-SYLVANER AFTER THE TWO VARIETIES FROM WHICH HERR MULLER OF THURGAU CREATED HIS CROSS.

EVIDENCE OF A WINE'S NEW ZEALAND HERITAGE CAN OCCASIONALLY BE DISCERNED IN PLACE-NAMES WHICH DERIVE FROM MAORIE. NOTABLE AMONG THESE IS TE KAUWHATA, ONE OF THE BEST KNOWN — IF NOT THE BEST — VINEYARD REGIONS.

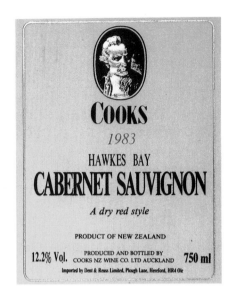

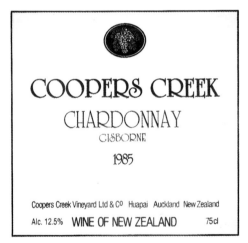

Yugoslav names such as Babich and Selaks are frequently used by New Zealand producers as many of the first winegrowers were Dalmatian immigrants. Cooks is one of New Zealand's largest wine companies, named after the British seafarer; Hawkes Bay and Gisborne are two of the country's best wine growing regions.

SOUTH AFRICA

*S*INCE 1972, SOUTH AFRICAN WINES HAVE CARRIED DISTINCTIVE SEALS OF ORIGIN: SEALS WITH BLUE BANDS MERELY SHOW THAT A WINE HAS BEEN CERTIFIED, RED BANDS SHOW THE CERTIFICATION OF THE VINTAGE, AND GREEN BANDS INDICATE THE CERTIFICATION OF THE "CULTIVAR", OR GRAPE VARIETY. AS ELSEWHERE A LITTLE LEEWAY IS ALLOWED, WITH WINES LABELLED CABERNET SAUVIGNON, FOR EXAMPLE, HAVING TO CONTAIN AT LEAST 80% OF THAT VARIETY. "SUPERIOR" WINE IS 100% WHAT IT SAYS IT IS. FORTY INDIVIDUAL PROPERTIES ARE ALLOWED TO DESCRIBE THEMSELVES ON THE LABEL AS ESTATES, THIS BEING LIMITED TO BOTTLED WINE MADE FROM GRAPES THEY HAVE GROWN THEMSELVES. COOPERATIVES CONTROL A LARGE PROPORTION OF WINE PRODUCTION.

SOUTH AFRICAN LABELS CAN BE CONFUSING AS GRAPE NAMES CAN BE QUITE BIZARRE. THE CHENIN BLANC IS KNOWN AS THE STEEN. SIMPLE ENOUGH, BUT HOW DOES THE "HERMITAGE" — THE NAME USED BY THE AUSTRALIANS FOR THE SYRAH — COME TO BE THE SOUTH AFRICAN NAME FOR CINSAULT? AND HOW DOES THE MOST SPANISH OF ALL VARIETIES, THE PALOMINO, COME TO BE CALLED THE "FRENCH GRAPE"? OTHER ODD GRAPE NAMES ARE THE HANEPOOT, FOR MUSCAT OF ALEXANDRIA, AND GREEN GRAPE FOR SEMILLON.

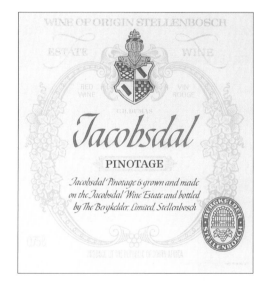

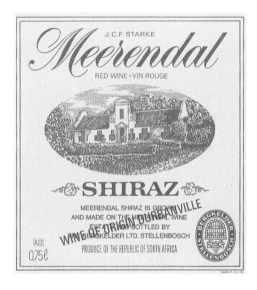

Grünberger is a trademark, whereas Stein indicates that the wine is made from the Chenin Blanc grape. Jacobsdal is an estate with the wine being made from the Pinotage, a cross between the Pinot Noir and Shiraz. Fleur du Cap is a commercial brand which, like others here, hopes to gain from a French image. The Meerendal Shiraz was bottled by the Bergkelder Ltd Cooperative.

OTHER COUNTRIES

*M*OVING AWAY FROM THE COUNTRIES WHOSE WINES HAVE THE LONGEST TRADITION OF WINE BOTTLING AND LABELLING, AND THOSE WHICH HAVE ACHIEVED INTERNATIONAL SALES FOR MANY OF THEIR WINES ALTHOUGH NEW TO THE GAME, IT CLEARLY BECOMES DANGEROUS TO GENERALIZE.

HOWEVER, WHILE TRADITIONAL WINE PRODUCERS FROM CYPRUS TO THE CRIMEA HAVE CONTINUED TO USE THE STYLES OF LABELS THEIR GREAT GRANDPARENTS MIGHT RECOGNIZE, THERE HAS BEEN AN INTERNATIONAL TENDENCY TO COPY FRENCH LABELS. THE PLETHORA OF *CHATEAU* LABELS WHICH HAVE FEATURED ON SOME VERY SURPRISING BOTTLES IS JUST ONE FEATURE OF THIS TREND ALTHOUGH SOMETIMES, AS IN THE CASE OF NORTH AFRICA, THERE ARE HISTORICAL LINKS WITH FRANCE WHICH MAKE SUCH LABELLING VERY UNDERSTANDABLE.

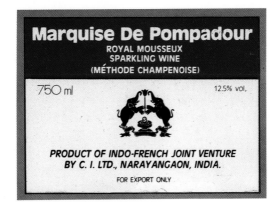

Eastern European labels are seldom dynamic and eye-catching although this Yugoslavian label from Kastalet tries hard. Lutomer Riesling is very popular in the English-speaking world, even though it is unrelated to the great Riesling grown in Germany. The Marquise de Pompadour is a first effort at sparkling wine — and labelling — in India: the wine is better than the label.

ABOVE: The Concha y Toro from Chile has a little plastic Satan attached to every bottle. The Argentinian Franchette label is a collector's item, removed from one of the last bottles to be imported into Britain before the Falkland Islands war. The Commanderie St. John label refers to Cyprus' crusading history, while the Greek Château Carras label tries very hard to seem French, and is "Mis en Bouteille au Château". OPPOSITE: The Rumanian Muscat Ottonel label is both traditional and effectively commercial.

THEMES

OVER THE YEARS, WINEMAKERS THROUGHOUT THE WORLD HAVE PROVED EXTRAORDINARILY IMAGINATIVE IN THE WAYS IN WHICH THEY HAVE LABELLED THEIR WINE. HOW MUCH OF THIS SPRINGS FROM CONTRACTED DESIGNERS, AND HOW MUCH FROM THE WINEMAKERS THEMSELVES IS DIFFICULT TO SAY, BUT IT IS CLEAR THAT TODAY, LABEL DESIGN IS MORE IMPORTANT THAN IT HAS EVER BEEN.

ON STUDYING THE THOUSANDS OF LABELS ASSEMBLED FOR THIS BOOK, A NUMBER OF THEMES EMERGED, SOME OF WHICH WERE QUITE SURPRISING. CLAUDE CLEVENOT'S FLORAL LABELS FOR GEORGES DUBOEUF, FOR EXAMPLE, WERE FAR FROM THE FIRST TO ASSOCIATE FLOWERS WITH WINE, BUT THEY WERE THE FIRST TO MAKE A TRULY INTERNATIONAL IMPACT. NOT ONLY COULD ONE WINE PRODUCER'S LABELS BE RECOGNISED INSTANTLY, BUT ALSO PEOPLE WHO HAD NEVER TASTED DUBOEUF'S WINES COULD, JUST BY LOOKING AT THEIR LABELS, GUESS AT THEIR FRUITINESS.

OTHER WINEMAKERS AND LABEL DESIGNERS HAVE EXPLORED DIFFERENT THEMES, RANGING FROM THE OVERTLY "ARTY" AND THE ABSTRACT, TO THE HUMOROUS AND THE ELABORATELY "OLDE-WORLDE". SOMETIMES THESE LABELS DO APTLY CONVEY THE STYLE OF BOTH THE WINE AND ITS PRODUCER, BUT AT OTHERS THEY ARE UNINTENTIONALLY COMICAL OR JUST PLAIN SPURIOUS.

VINEYARDS

*T*HE APPEAL OF DEPICTING VINEYARDS ON WINE LABELS
IS OBVIOUS; SADLY THEY ARE OFTEN DULL, LOOKING AS
THOUGH THEY ARE ROUGH PROOFS TACKED TOGETHER
BY AN ADVERTISING AGENCY. THIS SELECTION OF VINE-
YARD LABELS, HOWEVER, USES A VARIETY OF STYLES TO
ILLUSTRATE THE WIDELY DIFFERING PIECES OF LAND IN
WHICH EACH OF THEIR WINES WERE PRODUCED.

THE
FIRESTONE
VINEYARD
Santa Ynez Valley

Johannisberg Riesling

Residual Sugar 2.45° BRIX   1985   Harvest Sugar 21.8° BRIX

Grown, Produced, and Bottled by The Firestone Vineyard
Los Olivos, California, U.S.A. · Bonded Winery No.4720
Alcohol 10.8% By Volume

EARLY HARVEST
Joseph Phelps Vineyards
1985

Napa Valley
Johannisberg Riesling

Alcohol 11.1% by volume
Sugar at harvest 19.5% by weight. Residual sugar 1.2% by weight.
Produced and bottled by Joseph Phelps Vineyards, St. Helena, Ca.

CHINON
DOMAINE DE LA NOBLAIE
11,5°/% vol   APPELLATION CHINON CONTROLÉE   75 cl
PIERRE MANZAGOL Propriétaire-viticulteur · DOMAINE DE LA NOBLAIE · 37500 LIGRÉ
mis en bouteille à la propriété

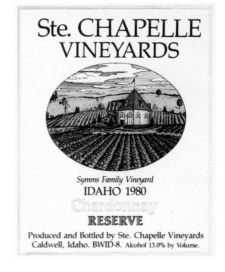

Ste. CHAPELLE
VINEYARDS

Symms Family Vineyard
IDAHO 1980
Chardonnay
RESERVE

Produced and Bottled by Ste. Chapelle Vineyards
Caldwell, Idaho. BWID-8. Alcohol 13.0% by Volume.

These three American labels — two from California, one from Idaho —
complement the very typically French label from Chinon in the Loire.

This set of labels illustrates as well as any textbook the variety of the world's vineyards. The Cabernet del Poggio in Italy and the Clos St. Hune from Alsace in France, are both from vines planted on fairly steep slopes. The Domaine La Fourmone (the strange language on this label is the regional dialect) and Mas de Daumas Gassac are flatter vineyards, but very different in style from the apparently forest-edged Californian Château Rutherford and Sycamore Creek. As for Gravelly Creek, it is easy to see how this vineyard got its name; the Cabernet Sauvignon traditionally likes being planted in gravelly soil.

CHATEAU RUTHERFORD
1977

SPECIAL RV RESERVE

NAPA VALLEY

Cabernet Sauvignon

Alcohol 12% By Volume

Produced & Bottled By Rutherford Vintners,
Rutherford, Napa County, California B.W. 4805

Sycamore Creek
1981
California
CARIGNANE
Estate Bottled

PRODUCED AND BOTTLED BY SYCAMORE CREEK VINEYARDS
MORGAN HILL, CALIFORNIA   ALCOHOL 12.5% BY VOLUME

diamond creek

Gravelly Meadow

Napa **1980** Valley

Cabernet Sauvignon

grown, produced and bottled on diamond mountain by

DIAMOND CREEK VINEYARDS   CALISTOGA, CA.

ALCOHOL 12½% BY VOLUME

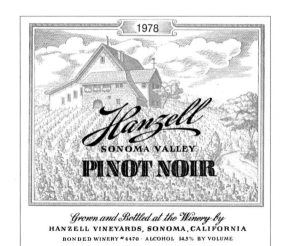

1978

Hanzell
SONOMA VALLEY
PINOT NOIR

Grown and Bottled at the Winery by
HANZELL VINEYARDS, SONOMA, CALIFORNIA
BONDED WINERY #4470 · ALCOHOL 14.5% BY VOLUME

C E L L A R S
&
B A R R E L S

*G*IVEN THE FACT THAT MOST WINE SPENDS AT LEAST PART
OF ITS LIFE IN A CELLAR OF SOME KIND OR ANOTHER, CEL-
LARS AND BARRELS FEATURE LESS IN LABEL DESIGNS
THAN ONE MIGHT EXPECT. WHEN THEY DO, IT EITHER
INVOLVES A PHOTOGRAPH (USUALLY DARK GREY ON PALE
GREY IN A SMALL OVAL SHAPE) OR A CRUDE WOODCUT
DEPICTING A FEW CASKS. HOWEVER, SORTING THROUGH
THE LABELS I HAD COLLECTED WHICH INVOLVED EITHER
CELLARS OR BARRELS, I FOUND GREATER ORIGINALITY
THAN I HAD ANTICIPATED.

VINTAGE 1981	BOTTLED APRIL 1985
Bottle	of a total of 34,956 Bottles
Magnum	of a total of 1,200 Magnums

Heitz Cellar

NAPA VALLEY
CABERNET SAUVIGNON
ALCOHOL 13½% BY VOLUME
 PRODUCED AND BOTTLED IN OUR CELLAR BY
HEITZ WINE CELLARS
ST. HELENA, CALIFORNIA, U.S.A.

BARBERA d'ASTI

VIVACE
DENOMINAZIONE DI ORIGINE CONTROLLATA
Prodotto ed imbottigliato dall'Azienda Agricola
GALLONE FRANCESCO - CANELLI (Asti)
Reg. Monforte, 150 - Tel. (0141) 83.44.10
Lt. 0,750   R. I. V. 108/AT   Alcool eff. 12,5% vol.

Although the wines could hardly be more different, there is an obvious visual link between the label of Heitz Cellar's Californian Cabernet Sauvignon and that of a wine made from the Barbera grape in Italy. Note the small Martha's Vineyard at the bottom left-hand corner of the Heitz wine, indicating that this bottle comes from one of California's very best vineyards.

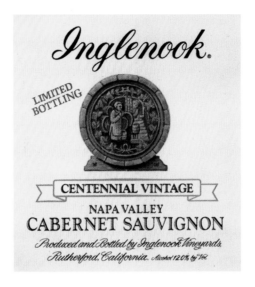

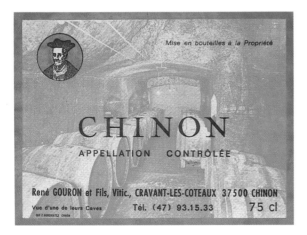

*The jokey Boskydel label from Michigan is a nicely tongue-in-cheek
counterpart to the Inglenook from California. Both stand firmly apart from
the very traditional French Chinon and Chablis labels with their classic
depictions of cellars.*

CASTLES
&
HERALDRY

*I*T IS HARDLY SURPRISING THAT CASTLES AND HERALDRY PLAY SUCH A SIGNIFICANT PART IN WINE LABEL DESIGN. AFTER ALL, HISTORICALLY, A MAJOR PART OF WINE PRODUCTION HAS ALWAYS BEEN UNDER THE CONTROL OF THE ARISTOCRACY — ALTHOUGH NOWADAYS ONE SHOULD AVOID THE TRAP OF ASSUMING THAT GREAT AMOUNTS OF WINE OUTSIDE OF BORDEAUX ARE CHATEAUX PRODUCED. THE NEXT FEW PAGES ILLUSTRATE LABELS WHICH USE THE THEMES WITH EITHER ORIGINALITY OR STYLE — OR BOTH.

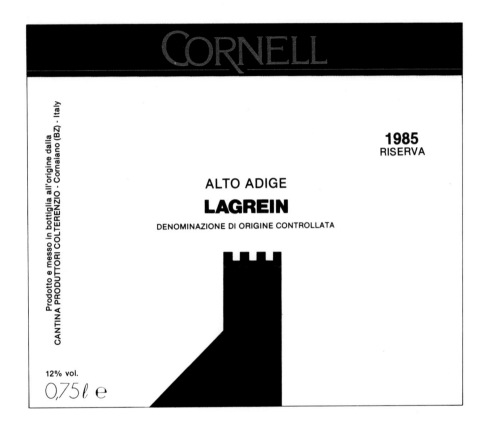

This is one of my favourite labels, thanks to its simplicity. The wine, made from the Lagrein grape, comes from the Alto Adige in Italy.

French castles range from the classically palatial Château St. Georges (it really does look like this) to the more medieval Châteaux Olivier and de Beaune. Others castles include the Castello della Sala in Italy, the more tongue-in-cheek Castle Cary in England, Château Montelina in California and the Italian Castel S. Michele. The Castillo de Tebas from Navarra in Spain, however, does appear to be seriously pretentious.

CASTLE CARY
ENGLISH TABLE WINE
75cl   MÜLLER-THURGAU & SEYVAL BLANC   75cl

Bottled for Mr & Mrs Woosnam Mills of Castle Cary Vineyard,
Castle Cary, Somerset by W1296

CHATEAU
MONTELENA
1882 - 1982
CENTENNIAL

NAPA VALLEY
Cabernet Sauvignon
ESTATE 1978 BOTTLED

GROWN, PRODUCED & BOTTLED BY CHATEAU MONTELENA
WINERY • CALISTOGA, NAPA VALLEY, CALIFORNIA
ALCOHOL 14.3% BY VOLUME

castel s.michele
VINO DA TAVOLA DI S. MICHELE a/A

75 CL.   Reg. N. 767/TN   12,20 % VOL.

Imbottigliato da: ISTITUTO AGRARIO PROVINCIALE S. MICHELE a A (Italia)

botella
N° E 033020

Reserva 1976
Castillo
de
Tiebas

Esta gran reserva se elabora solo en años excepcionales con cepas
Tempranillo y Garnacho. La cosecha de 1976 ha producido 157.200
botellas bordelesas y 7.200 magnums de vino criado en las barricas de roble
y en los añejos de nuestra centenaria bodega de Las Campanas

vino de Navarra
Bodega Vinicola Navarra
fundada en 1880

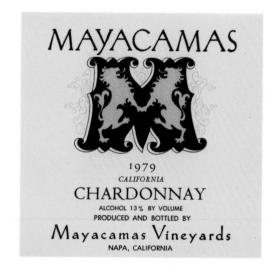

Coats of arms of every kind — and a bit of a cheat from California. My own favourite is probably the Monprivato Barolo which seems to be a classy label overall. The Graacher Himmelreich and the Sauvignon de St. Bris, from the Mosel and northern Burgundy respectively, are very typical of their regional labelling styles. The Soave and the Spanna are examples of overdoing a good thing.

FLOWERS

FLOWERS HAVE APPEARED ON LABELS SINCE THE EARLIEST DAYS OF LABEL DESIGN, USUALLY IN THE FORM OF GARLANDS AND BOUQUETS. THE IDEA OF CREATING A FLORAL IMAGE FOR THE WHOLE LABEL IS MORE UNUSUAL AND — IF ONE SETS ASIDE THE PAINTED FLOWERS THAT GALLE PUT ON THE PERRIER JOUET CHAMPAGNE BOTTLES, AND WHICH HAVE REAPPEARED ON THAT COMPANY'S BELLE EPOQUE BOTTLES TODAY — THE ONE COMPANY WHICH SEEMS TO HAVE MADE FLOWERS THEIR OWN IS DUBOEUF. BOTH CHAMPAGNE AND BEAUJOLAIS ARE IDEALLY SUITED TO FLOWERS AND FLORAL IMAGES, AS ARE MANY OF THE OTHER WINES WHICH HAVE FOLLOWED IN THE WAKE OF THESE TWO PIONEERING TYPES OF WINE. THERE CAN BE FEW BETTER WAYS TO GIVE THE IMPRESSION OF A FRESH, EMPHATICALLY FRUITY WINE. HOWEVER, THERE HAVE BEEN ATTEMPTS TO PRINT PICTURES OF FLOWERS ON THE LABELS OF BIG, BEEFY RED WINES WHICH, TO MY MIND AT LEAST, DESTROYS THE WHOLE OBJECT OF CHOOSING THIS KIND OF IMAGE IN THE FIRST PLACE.

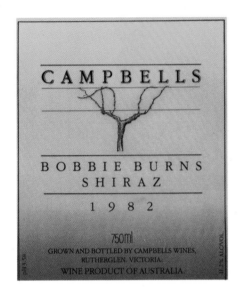

*Vines, both in leaf and in a more wintery state, feature on labels from
Australia and the US; the Bollini label, by contrast, favours an amalgam of
flowers and musical instruments in an attempt at a Renaissance style.*

ABOVE: Flowers also appear in original styles in California and Italy, though quite why a black rose should be thought appropriate to rosé is hard to imagine — perhaps it is a joke. OPPOSITE: Unquestionably the most famous flower label designs of all are those for the Duboeuf Beaujolais.

D E S I G N

*B*Y THEIR VERY NATURE, WINE LABELS OUGHT TO HAVE
ATTRACTED SOME OF THE MOST INNOVATIVE DESIGN IN THE
WORLD. IN SOME COUNTRIES, MOST NOTABLY ITALY, THE
UNITED STATES AND AUSTRALIA, THIS IS PRECISELY WHAT
HAS HAPPENED. ELSEWHERE AN INGRAINED REVERENCE
FOR TRADITION, AND PERHAPS FOR WINE ITSELF, SEEMS TO
HAVE INHIBITED THE PROCESS. IT IS PERHAPS FOR THIS
REASON THAT SO FEW OF THE LABELS WHICH APPEAR IN
THIS SECTION ARE FROM THE MORE FAMILIAR OF EUR-
OPE'S WINEMAKING REGIONS.

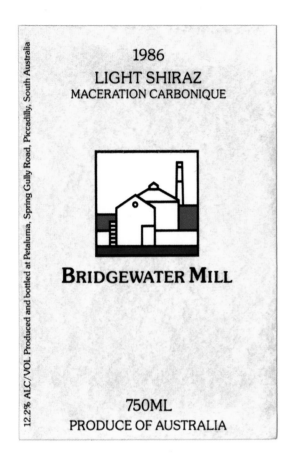

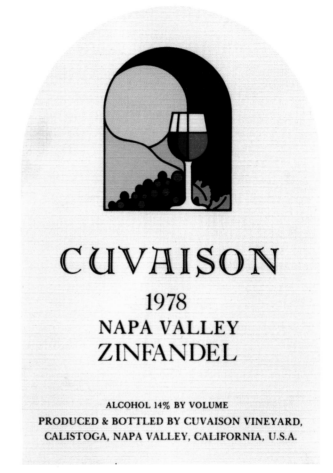

When designing a label, the challenge is to create a style which complements rather than competes with the character of the wine. This pair, from California and Australia respectively, grace a rather full-bodied and a fresh, fruity wine. Without a helpful, descriptive text, the difference in style would not necessarily be immediately apparent. Macération Carbonique refers to a Beaujolais style of winemaking.

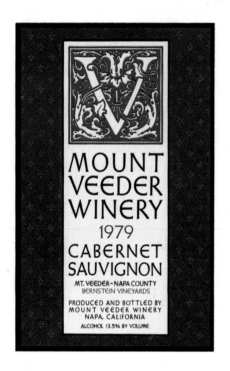

ABOVE: Attractive labels which seem to make reference to wallpaper and fabric. OPPOSITE: The Cloudy Bay label is quite simply one of the best in the world. (The wine is pretty good too...)

Three Beaujolais labels from three different producers, but by the same label printer, Claude Clevenot. Compare these with Clevenot's floral Beaujolais labels for Duboeuf (p109) and the traditional Morgon label on page 38. All of these designs are perfect labels for a fresh, easy-to-gulp wine which, after all, is what Beaujolais ought to be.

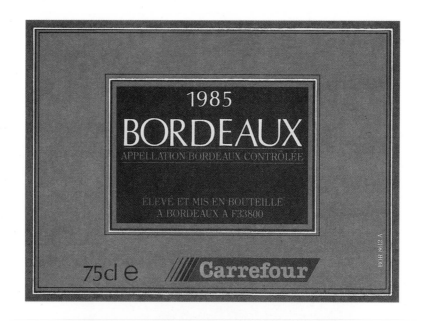

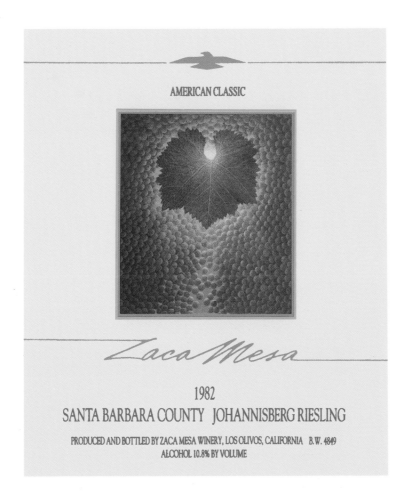

AMERICAN CLASSIC

Zaca Mesa

1982
SANTA BARBARA COUNTY   JOHANNISBERG RIESLING

PRODUCED AND BOTTLED BY ZACA MESA WINERY, LOS OLIVOS, CALIFORNIA   B.W. 4849
ALCOHOL 10.8% BY VOLUME

*Designers are very clearly at work here on the Carrefour Bordeaux label
which is unusually classy for an own-label wine sold by a French
supermarket chain, and a simple Ribolla Gialla label from Italy. The
American Classic label is a classic piece of design.*

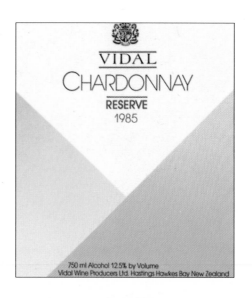

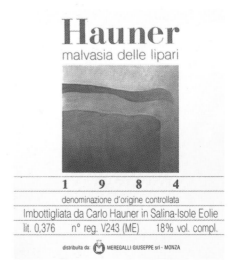

ABOVE: A set of labels which use colour very effectively. The Vidal is one of the most original in New Zealand and the Mâcon is very unusual, given the conservative nature of this region. The two Italian labels are less surprising, but both are among the most effective that this design-conscious country has produced. OPPOSITE: The Rothbury Estate label proves that simple use of silver can achieve as great an impact as any amount of colour.

The Sparkling Far Niente and Starwine labels are wonderful examples of design gone crazy, strangely evocative of glossy children's book illustrations rather than wine labels. The Italian Il Grigio, the Mondavi and the Chez Panisse labels impress, too, with the cleanness of their designs, although any of these could just as easily appear on a bottle of scent as on a bottle of wine. But how much does that really matter? White Zinfandel, incidentally, means pink Zinfandel.

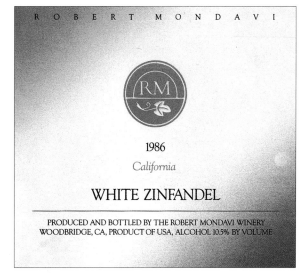

A R T

S PECIALLY COMMISSIONED ART IS USED INCREASINGLY IN WINE LABEL DESIGNS. THE TREND WAS ESTABLISHED BY BARON PHILIPPE DE ROTHSCHILD MORE THAN 60 YEARS AGO WHEN HE COMMISSIONED THE WELL-KNOWN POSTER DESIGNER, CARLU, TO DESIGN A MOUTON ROTHSCHILD LABEL TODAY, MANY WINEMAKERS HAVE FOLLOWED HIS EXAMPLE, PARTICULARLY IN THE UNITED STATES AND AUSTRALIA.

*A set of specially-commissioned labels from an up-and-coming champagne
house, looking reminiscent of Mouton Rothschild's labels.*

ABOVE: Is this art? It may not be but it is certainly one of the most unusual and dramatic labels around. OPPOSITE: A selection of labels, each of which has made use of a painting or illustration. My own favourite is the Heggies Vineyard label from Australia.

Stark's Star

A NATURAL DESSERT WINE
ALCOHOL 16% BY VOLUME
PRODUCED AND BOTTLED BY MOUNT PLEASANT VINEYARDS
AUGUSTA, MISSOURI

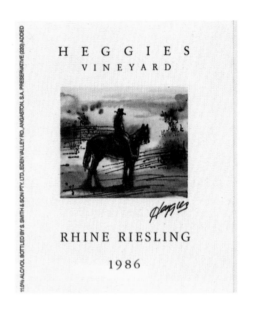

HEGGIES
VINEYARD

RHINE RIESLING

1986

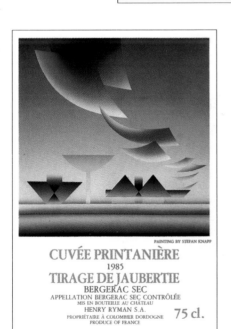

PAINTING BY STEFAN KNAPP

CUVÉE PRINTANIÈRE
1985
TIRAGE DE JAUBERTIE
BERGERAC SEC
APPELLATION BERGERAC SEC CONTRÔLÉE
MIS EN BOUTEILLE AU CHÂTEAU
HENRY RYMAN S.A.
PROPRIÉTAIRE À COLOMBIER DORDOGNE
PRODUCE OF FRANCE

75 cl.

«ESPERIT DE VI» Artista Rosélló

Mont-Marçal
Penedes

GRAN RESERVA ESPECIAL 1970
IMPORTEUR BARISI & CIE AG, BERN

Botella

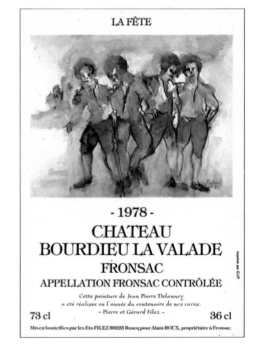

LA FÊTE

- 1978 -
CHATEAU
BOURDIEU LA VALADE
FRONSAC
APPELLATION FRONSAC CONTRÔLÉE

Cette peinture de Jean Pierre Delanney
a été réalisée en l'année du centenaire de nos caves.
- Pierre et Gérard Filez -

73 cl   36 cl

Mis en bouteilles par les Ets FILEZ 89223 Roncq pour Alain ROUX, propriétaire à Fronsac.

Drapeau   Willem Snitker
Cuvée Spéciale
mis en bouteille au Château par René Mazeau
Propriétaire à Targon (Gironde)
Tirage limité

CHATEAU
TOUTIGEAC
1984
BORDEAUX
APPELLATION BORDEAUX CONTROLEE
RENE MAZEAU, Propriétaire à TARGON - France
Cette bouteille porte le
PRODUCE OF FRANCE
MEDAILLE D'OR
FRANCE
75cl e
Alc. 12 %

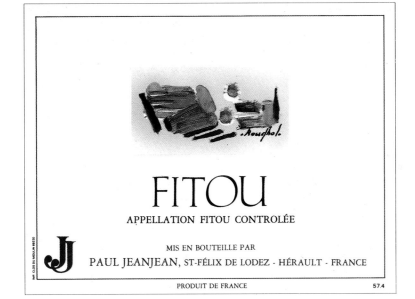

FITOU
APPELLATION FITOU CONTROLÉE

MIS EN BOUTEILLE PAR
PAUL JEANJEAN, ST-FÉLIX DE LODEZ - HÉRAULT - FRANCE

PRODUIT DE FRANCE   57.4

*Even more labels inspired by Mouton Rothschild, particularly in the case of
Château Toutigeac and the Rioja, with each of the labels using an abstract
image to achieve an effect.*

In order to understand the step that Baron Philippe de Rothschild took when putting art — not to mention modern art — on the labels of his wine, one has to understand both the nature of the man and of the highly conservative region in which he inherited his vineyards.

From the outset Rothschild was unconventional and flamboyant. As a young man, he raced cars against professionals, became involved in the theatre and befriended a range of Paris-based artists. So it was hardly surprising that he chose to use a poster designer called Carlu to design his 1924 label, loudly proclaiming that the entire production of the château was bottled on site.

Rothschild's real excursion into using artists began after the war in 1945. Since then, the tradition of employing a different artist every year has been steadily maintained, with the exception of 1977 — a tribute to Queen Elizabeth the Queen Mother, who must have wished she had graced a better vintage. Other wineries throughout the world have since followed Rothschild's example.

*A selection of Mouton Rothschild labels, including the 1973 label which was
based on an existing Picasso painting from the Baron's own collection.*

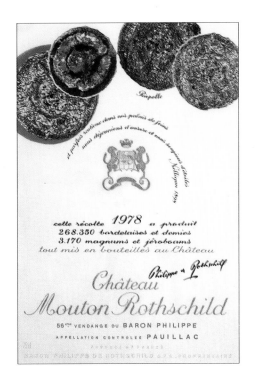

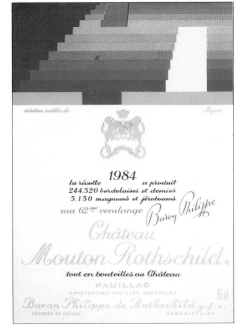

M A P S

*T*HERE ARE, IN FACT, VERY FEW LABELS THAT INCLUDE
MAPS AS A MAJOR PART OF THEIR DESIGN, BUT I HAVE PUT
THIS COLLECTION TOGETHER WITH THE THOUGHT THAT
THEY MIGHT DENOTE SOME KIND OF LABELLING TREND IN
THE FUTURE. AS BACK LABELS BECOME MORE VERBOSE,
THE ANSWER MIGHT BE TO START PUTTING USEFUL IN-
FORMATION BACK ON THE FRONT LABEL.

*None of the four map labels here has used any kind of serious modern
cartography, preferring to concentrate on either real or old maps. Of these,
the most impressive is the Bom Retiro which includes a classic map of the
Douro River.*

Beaulieu Vineyard

LOS CARNEROS REGION
NAPA VALLEY
Pinot Noir

BV.

PRODUCED AND BOTTLED BY BEAULIEU VINEYARD
RUTHERFORD, NAPA COUNTY, CALIFORNIA   ALCOHOL 13.5% BY VOL.

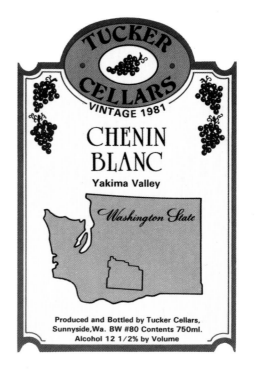

CHENIN
BLANC

Yakima Valley

Produced and Bottled by Tucker Cellars,
Sunnyside, Wa. BW #80 Contents 750ml.
Alcohol 12 1/2% by Volume

Quinta do Bom-Retiro
PORTO
20 years

ADRIANO RAMOS-PINTO   V. N. DE GAIA - PORTUGAL
MATURED IN WOOD

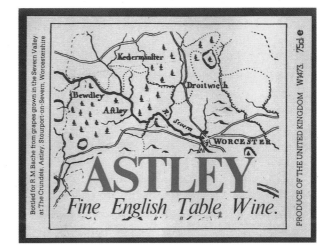

ASTLEY
Fine English Table Wine.

PEOPLE

*P*EOPLE DO NOT SEEM TO FEATURE ON LABELS AS MUCH AS THEY MIGHT AND INDEED, WHEN THEY DO, THE REASONS ARE OFTEN RATHER UNCONVINCING. THE FOLLOWING LABELS, HOWEVER, USE IMAGES OF HUMAN BEINGS MORE INTERESTINGLY AND, IN ONE OR TWO CASES, RATHER SURPRISINGLY.

The familiar face on the Guenoc label is that of Lillie Langtry who established a winery in Jersey; the rather less lovely Jean Descombes is one of the best winemakers in the Beaujolais. The Chianti lady is married to the winemaker, and there is good reason for featuring Napoleon on a Corsican wine label because he was born on the island. Close examination of the label of Langan's Brasserie's house wine reveals the presence of a young-looking Michael Caine, seated beside Richard Sheppard, Langan's chef, and Langan himself. Caine is one of the restaurant's owners.

ABOVE: One of my very favourite labels from Schloss Vollrads in Germany manages to bring an element of rare humour to a label of what is, in fact, a very serious wine. OPPOSITE: Alexis Chanson was the founder of the firm of Chanson, and Josephine Doré was the French-born grandmother of Marco di Bartoli to whom this Marsala maker dedicated his wine.

Guenoc

1980
North Coast
Chardonnay

Produced and Bottled by Guenoc Cellar
St. Helena, California Alcohol 13.9% by volume

MORGON
APPELLATION CONTRÔLÉE

75 cl

PRODUCED AND BOTTLED IN FRANCE
Sélectionné et mis en bouteille au domaine par
LES VINS GEORGES DUBŒUF ROMANÈCHE-THORINS 71

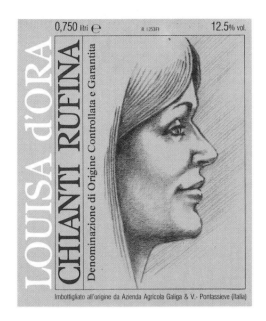

0,750 litri ℮   R.1253/FI   12.5% vol.

LOUISA d'ORA
CHIANTI RUFINA
Denominazione di Origine Controllata e Garantita
Imbottigliato all'origine da Azienda Agricola Galiga & V.- Pontassieve (Italia)

CAP CORSE
BIANCO

100 cl   15% vol.

CAP CORSE AU QUINQUINA

L:N. MATTEI

SOCIÉTÉ DES VINS DU CAP CORSE
20290 BORGO BASTIA

*The familiar face on the Guenoc label is that of Lillie Langtry who
established a winery in Jersey; the rather less lovely Jean Descombes is one
of the best winemakers in the Beaujolais. The Chianti lady is married to the
winemaker, and there is good reason for featuring Napoleon on a Corsican
wine label because he was born on the island.*

A N I M A L S
&
B I R D S

A NIMALS OF ONE KIND OR ANOTHER SEEM TO BE
GROWING IN POPULARITY AMONG WINEMAKERS. BEASTS I
HAVE DISCOVERED AND REGRETFULLY EXCLUDED FROM
THESE PAGES HAVE INCLUDED A SPANIEL, A TURKEY AND A
FROG; I HAVE LITTLE DOUBT THAT FURTHER SEARCHES
WOULD LEAD TO FERRETS, SLUGS AND MAYBE COCK-
ROACHES. THE SELECTION WHICH FOLLOWS IS, HOWEVER,
REPRESENTATIVE OF THE VINOUS BESTIARY AS A WHOLE,
AND THE EVIDENT AFFECTION FOR BIRDS, IN PARTICULAR.

IMBOTTIGLIATO DA VIETTI CASTIGLIONE FALLETTO ITALIA
ANNATA 1986

Vietti

DOLCETTO D'ALBA

DENOMINAZIONE DI ORIGINE CONTROLLATA
DELLA LOCALITA' BUSSIA
DELLE 6805 BOTTIGLIE QUESTA E' LA

R.I. 220 / CN
disegno di claudio bonichi

75 cl. e

12,00% VOL.
stampatore gianni cozzo

Dogs chasing birds frequently seem to feature on Italian labels.

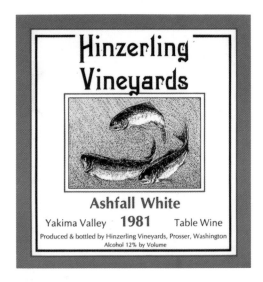

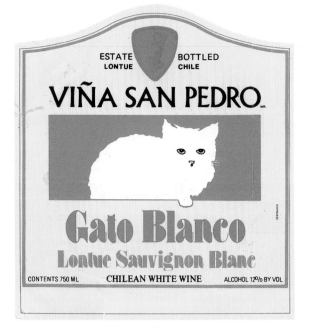

ABOVE: While retaining a special affection for the Chilean white cat, I think this label is very silly indeed. The Washington fish, the New York State otter and the Devon deer somehow manage to add an incongruous touch of class to their labels. OPPOSITE: Birds in New York State, Oregon and Tuscany.

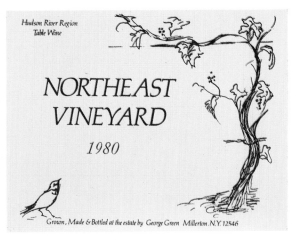

PAINTED
&
SANDBLASTED

WHILE THE VAST MAJORITY OF WINE BOTTLES ARE STILL PRESENTED WITH PAPER LABELS, THERE HAS BEEN A GROWING TREND TOWARDS PRINTING LABELS DIRECTLY ONTO GLASS, OR USING MATERIALS OTHER THAN PAPER. A SANDPAPER LABEL APPEARS ON PAGE 143; THE FOLLOWING SELECTION CAN BE CONSIDERED ALONGSIDE THAT LABEL AS AN INTERESTING OBJECT LESSON IN HOW TO MAKE A BOTTLE STAND OUT FROM THE CROWD.

The familiar Belle Epoque label used by Perrier Jouët for one of its prestigious champagnes is a perfect replica of a bottle designed in 1920 by the glass artist Emile Gallé, five of which were discovered accidentally in the company's cellars in 1969.

ABOVE: Portugal is the home of the cork tree and of bottle cork production, so it is hardly surprising that it has come up with a cork label. Might this be the only wine in the world to give off a "corky" smell before it has been attacked with a corkscrew? *OPPOSITE:* An unusual example of a label printed on sandpaper for a go-ahead German estate.

W O R D S

*T*O SEPARATE LABELS WHOSE DESIGNS DEPEND ON TYPOGRAPHY MIGHT SEEM A SLIGHTLY STRANGE CHOICE, BUT IT BECAME APPARENT THAT THERE IS A VERY DEFINITE SCHOOL OF TYPOGRAPHICAL — AND SOMETIMES HAND-WRITTEN — LABELLING WHICH USES THE WINE NAME AND INFORMATION ABOUT IT TO CREATE A DESIGN.

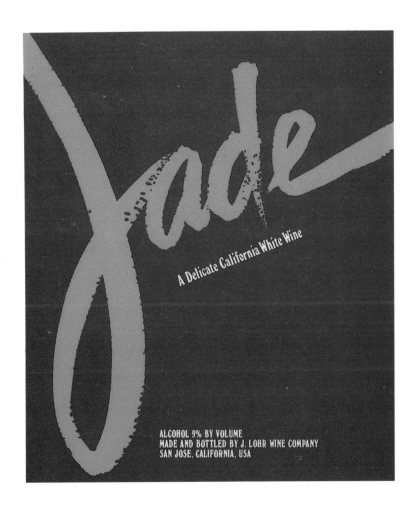

This Jade label is a perfect example of a label which relies totally on the impact of the wine name. The style works well, although whether the boldness of the wording is entirely appropriate to what is described as a "delicate white wine" is questionable.

Produce of France   Récolte   1982

Beaujolais Morgon

Appellation Contrôlée

Mis en bouteilles à Graves/Anse
pour J.B.Reynier – London–SW1
70 cl   par C.V.C. 63653

Zinfandel
AMADOR COUNTY

Our 1980 Amador Zinfandel consists
of 29.6% Petit Sirah and 70.4%
Amador Zinfandel. The Petit Sirah
gave the Zinfandel the middle body it
needed, while retaining the immense
and exciting fruit of Zinfandel.

This wine will please those looking for
rich, flavorful drinking or short-term
(3 to 5 years) bottle aging.

Please call for an appointment:
(408) 354-4214

David Bruce

VINTAGE 1980

Zinfandel

AMADOR COUNTY

Produced & Bottled by David Bruce
Los Gatos, California
Alcohol 14.1% by Volume

*The Beaujolais Margon and the Zinfandel are two examples of labels which
use an apparently handwritten style for effect. Ridge makes bold use of a
plain, modern style of print to indicate provenance, grape, producer and
vintage with almost unbeatable clarity. Mount Hope and the Portuguese
João Pires are rather fussier in their style. The Le Vigne San Petro Refola is
a good example of an essentially modern-style Italian table wine making
use of a mock-medieval label, quite successfully.*

80 Zinfandel, York Creek, Bottled May 1982
This full, berry flavored Zinfandel has the acid and tannin to make it a wine for aging. The excellent Petite Sirah grown at York Creek is mixed in the vineyard with part of the Zinfandel and the two are fermented together. The wine is clearly in the rich claret tradition for which we strive. Its complexity, as it develops, will come from the marriage of the two varieties, the full malolactic fermentation, and the extended aging in small oak cooperage. It should begin to open by next spring and develop with three or four years of bottle age. PD (3/82)

Begun in 1959, Ridge was one of the first of today's chateau-size California wineries, that is, those that attempt only the highest quality at the quantity levels of the classified chateaux (up to 40,000 cases). All the wines are aged in small oak cooperage with the majority receiving no cellar treatment other than racking. Located above 2300 feet on Monte Bello Ridge in the Santa Cruz Mountains, our winery and main vineyards overlook San Francisco Bay. For information on ordering wines or visiting us for tasting, please send a note or call (408) 867-3233. DRB (1/80)

PRODUCT OF CALIFORNIA, U.S.A.

RIDGE
CALIFORNIA
ZINFANDEL
YORK CREEK
1980

NET CONTENTS
750ML

SPRING MOUNTAIN, 90% ZINFANDEL, 10% PETITE SIRAH
FOOTHILLS NAPA COUNTY   ALCOHOL 13.9% BY VOLUME
PRODUCED AND BOTTLED BY RIDGE VINEYARDS, BW 4488
17100 MONTE BELLO RD, BOX AI, CUPERTINO, CALIFORNIA

Mount Hope
Mazza
Special Selection
Vidal Blanc
Pennsylvania
1982

A medium dry white wine. A Mazza Special Selection indicates that this bottling has met the Wine Master's strictest standards of excellence. 11% alcohol by volume. Produced and bottled by Mount Hope Estate & Winery. Manheim, Lancaster County, Pa. 17545

70 cl   11% alc./vol.

João Pires

Produce of Portugal
1985
White Palmela Wine

A refreshingly dry white wine produced from Muscat grapes grown in the Palmela region of Portugal, this wine is produced and bottled by João Pires & Filhos, Lda. - Pinhal Novo.

Sole Importers
Ehrmanns Wine Shippers Ltd.
London

LE VIGNE
DI
SAN PIERO

REFOLA'
Cabernet Sauvignon
di Sommacampagna
1985

Questo vino è stato imbottigliato all'origine dal viticoltore Franca Fiorio e prodotto con uve

coltivate esclusivamente nel proprio podere sito in località San Pietro di Sommacampagna.

Dell'annata sono state prodotte tremila duecentottanta bottiglie. Questa bottiglia porta il numero ....
vino da tavola
0,750 l e   Sommacampagna di Verona - Italia 12 % Vol.

VIDE

H U M O U R

H UMOUR — OR ATTEMPTS AT HUMOUR — MAKE RARE APPEARANCES ON WINE LABELS, PERHAPS BECAUSE WINE HAS ALWAYS BEEN TREATED WITH SUCH DEFERENCE AND RESPECT, AND PERHAPS ALSO BECAUSE MOST WOULD—BE HUMOROUS WINEMAKERS HAVE HAD SUFFICIENT SELF—CONTROL TO SAVE THE REST OF US FROM THEIR JOKES. THE FOLLOWING LABELS ARE A FEW OF THE ONES WHICH — FOR BETTER OR WORSE — WERE ALLOWED TO GET AWAY.

This book would not be complete without a label of the Cuvée des Humoristes — complete with mis-spelled "Costes du Rhône", though the bad taste of the La Gourmandise label has a quality all of its own. The goat definitely outclasses the rest and refers to the fact that Mr. Taylor, owner of the winery, is barred from using his own name on the labels.

ABOVE: *The bad taste of the* Cuvée Erotique *which, if it serves no other purpose, would be sure to offend both male wine bores and feminists. The Gai Vin label refers to the slogan "Small boys pee in water — drink wine instead".* OPPOSITE: *Someone must have thought the Barolo bottle and label a good idea.*

COMMEMORATIVE

*T*HE DESIGN DEFINITION OF A CLASSIC COMMEM-
ORATIVE WINE LABEL IS A LOOSE ONE. ON THE ONE HAND,
THERE ARE THE COMMEMORATED EVENTS OF GENUINE
RELEVANCE TO THE WINERY, WINE COMPANY OR WINE IN
QUESTION AND, ON THE OTHER, THERE ARE SHAMELESS
ATTEMPTS TO CASH IN ON EVENTS OR ANNIVERSARIES OF
WHICH WINE BUYERS MAY HAVE HEARD, BUT WHICH HAVE
NOTHING WHATSOEVER TO DO WITH THE WINE. THE UNITED
STATES BICENTENARY, FOR EXAMPLE, FEATURED ON ALL
KINDS OF LABELS.

English labels are so rarely interesting that it is particularly pleasant to be able to include this 1986 vintage example printed to celebrate the reappearance of Halley's Comet.

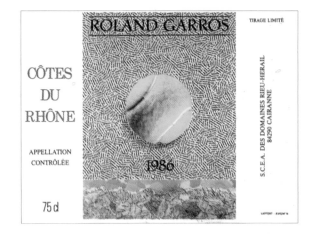

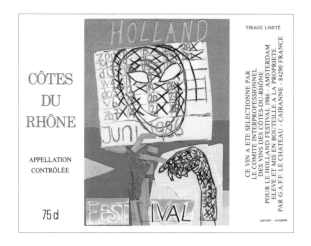

The *Côtes du Rhône* labels were produced for a number of international festivals by the winegrowers of that region who elect an official festival wine for each event after extensive blind tasting. Interestingly, all four of these were produced by the same estate, and all were made by an Englishman. The pair of labels commemorating the 1982 flight of the space shuttle have become collectors' items.

INDEX

Page numbers in *italic* refer to
the illustrations and captions